C I T Y P A C K
Paris

By Fiona Dunlop

3RD EDITION

Fodor's Travel Publications, Inc.
New York • Toronto • London • Sydney • Auckland

WWW.FODORS.COM

Contents

life **5–12**

INTRODUCING PARIS	6	A CHRONOLOGY	10
PARIS IN FIGURES	8	PEOPLE & EVENTS	
PARIS PEOPLE	9	FROM HISTORY	12

how to organize your time **13–22**

ITINERARIES	14	SIGHTSEEING TOURS	19
WALKS	16	EXCURSIONS	20
EVENING STROLLS	18	WHAT'S ON	22

top 25 sights **23–48**

1 MUSÉE MARMOTTAN	24	**14** JARDIN DU LUXEMBOURG	37
2 PALAIS DE CHAILLOT	25	**15** MUSÉE DE CLUNY	38
3 TOUR EIFFEL	26	**16** SAINTE CHAPELLE	39
4 CHAMPS ÉLYSÉES &		**17** CONCIERGERIE	40
ARC DE TRIOMPHE	27	**18** CENTRE GEORGES	
5 LES INVALIDES	28	POMPIDOU	41
6 MUSÉE RODIN	29	**19** MARCHÉ AUX PUCES DE	
7 PLACE DE LA CONCORDE	30	SAINT-OUEN	42
8 MUSÉE D'ORSAY	31	**20** NOTRE DAME	43
9 OPÉRA DE PARIS	32	**21** ÎLE SAINT-LOUIS	44
10 SACRÉ CŒUR	33	**22** INSTITUT DU MONDE	
11 MUSÉE DES ARTS		ARABE	45
DÉCORATIFS	34	**23** MUSÉE CARNAVALET	46
12 MUSÉE DU LOUVRE	35	**24** PLACE DES VOSGES	47
13 GALERIES VIVIENNE &		**25** CIMETIÈRE DU PÈRE	
COLBERT	36	LACHAISE	48

Index 94

About this book 4

best 49–60

MUSEUMS & GALLERIES	50	BRIDGES	55
PLACES OF WORSHIP	52	GREEN SPACES	56
CULT CAFÉS &		VIEWS	57
SALONS DE THÉ	53	CHILDREN'S ACTIVITIES	58
20TH-CENTURY		FREE ATTRACTIONS	59
ARCHITECTURE	54	INTRIGUING STREETS	60

where to... 61–86

STAY

LUXURY HOTELS	62		
MID-RANGE HOTELS	63		
BUDGET ACCOMMODATIONS	64		

EAT

EXPENSIVE RESTAURANTS	66
REGIONAL FRENCH	
RESTAURANTS	67
ASIAN RESTAURANTS	68
ARAB RESTAURANTS	69
ITALIAN & MISCELLANEOUS	
RESTAURANTS	70
BRASSERIES & BISTROS	72

SHOP

DEPARTMENT STORES	74
FOOD & WINE	75
MARKETS	76
ART & ANTIQUES	77
BOOKS & RECORDS	78
MISCELLANEOUS	79
FASHION	80

BE ENTERTAINED

CONCERTS, JAZZ CLUBS &	
NIGHTCLUBS	82
BARS & SPECIAL MOVIE	
THEATERS	84
SPORTS	86

travel facts 87–93

ARRIVING & DEPARTING	88	MEDIA & COMMUNICATIONS	91
ESSENTIAL FACTS	89	EMERGENCIES	92
PUBLIC TRANSPORTATION	90	LANGUAGE	93

CREDITS, ACKNOWLEDGMENTS, AND TITLES IN THIS SERIES   96

About this book

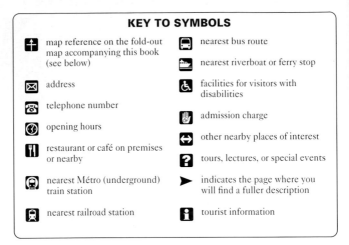

KEY TO SYMBOLS

✚ map reference on the fold-out map accompanying this book (see below)

⊠ address

☎ telephone number

🕐 opening hours

🍴 restaurant or café on premises or nearby

Ⓜ nearest Métro (underground) train station

🚉 nearest railroad station

🚌 nearest bus route

⛴ nearest riverboat or ferry stop

♿ facilities for visitors with disabilities

✋ admission charge

↔ other nearby places of interest

❓ tours, lectures, or special events

➤ indicates the page where you will find a fuller description

ℹ tourist information

Citypack Paris is divided into six sections to cover the six most important aspects of your visit to Paris. It includes:

- The author's view of the city and its people
- Itineraries, walks and excursions
- The top 25 sights to visit—as selected by the author
- Features on what makes the city special
- Detailed listings of restaurants, hotels, shops, and nightlife
- Practical information

In addition, easy-to-read side panels provide extra facts and snippets, highlights of places to visit, and invaluable practical advice.

CROSS-REFERENCES

To help you make the most of your visit, cross-references, indicated by ➤ , show you where to find additional information about a place or subject.

MAPS

The fold-out map in the wallet at the back of the book is a comprehensive street plan of Paris. All the map references given in the book refer to this map. For example, the Musée du Louvre at 99 rue de Rivoli has the following information: ✚ G5—indicating the grid square of the map in which the Musée du Louvre will be found.

The downtown maps found on the inside front and back covers of the book itself are for quick reference. They show the top 25 sights, described on pages 24–48, which are clearly plotted by number (❶ – ㉕ , not page number) from west to east across the city.

AREA CODE

French telephone numbers consist of ten digits and include the area code as the first two, with 01 as the code for Paris. If you call Paris from outside France, dial the country code (0033) then the subscriber number omitting the initial 0. To call a French number from within France simply dial the complete ten-digit number.

PARIS *life*

Introducing Paris	6
Paris in Figures	8
Paris People	9
A Chronology	10
People & Events from History	12

INTRODUCING PARIS

The French state

An unmistakable characteristic of France, and consequently Paris, is the state's top-heavy role. Which other industrialized country allows a state bank (Crédit Lyonnais) to run up losses approaching 60 billion FF (US $11 billion) in five years? And which other nation offers amnesty to all traffic offenders when a new president is elected?

Paris remains the powerhouse of the nation, despite repeated government maneuvers for decentralization. This is where French cultural trends are born, political battles are fielded, and national pride is polished. And yet it remains compact, still bordered by the *portes* (gateways) that keep the less prestigious *banlieues* (suburbs) at bay. Stay or live in central Paris and you are propelled into a maelstrom of gastronomy, fashion, cinema, art…and monuments. History is omnipresent and no ruler—whether king or president—has failed to leave his mark on the city.

Philosophy, ideas, and culture have long been favorite Parisian preoccupations, but at the turn of the 20th century the momentum is slowing. And while the capital still attracts many ambitious young provincials, the population is stagnating as more and more Parisians flee the ever-increasing pace of city life for a better quality of life in the suburbs or even further out. Yet, ironically, Paris has never been so beautiful: buildings erected as part of President Mitterrand's *grands projets* offer a stunning contrast to the wealth of renovated historic mansions. Spend a few days here and you cannot fail to be seduced by an enduring beauty, a grandeur, and a dynamism that few other capital cities combine.

Café life

Incomparable Paris

"Paris is complete, Paris is the ceiling of humankind...Whoever sees Paris thinks he sees the basis of all history with a sky and constellations in between. Paris is synonymous with the cosmos...it has no limits. Paris does more than make the law, it makes fashion. Paris can be stupid if it wants, it sometimes allows itself this luxury...It is more than great, it is immense. Why? Because it dares."

—Victor Hugo, *Les Misérables*.

Paris still harbors a fascinating cosmopolitan character. Stroll from one *quartier* to the next and you make a minor global tour, taking in Africa, Asia, the Caribbean, and the Arab world in Pigalle, Belleville or the 13th *arrondissement* (district). Plunge into the heart of the French bourgeois soul in the 7th or 16th *arrondissements*, or sweep up Parisian chic on the Left Bank. Stop at a café terrace to people-watch, read, or dream; wander along the *quais* or relax in a park.

Explore the Right Bank and you feel the capital's commercial pulse. Follow the city's cultural history in any of its numerous museums, catch up on new movies at the countless film theaters, or dive into a hot nightspot. But above all let the city lead you and do not believe the cliché that Parisians are unfriendly. Its winding streets hold surprises that even the most informative guidebook cannot cover, and it is only off the tourist beat that you encounter the true Parisian spirit.

The euro—a cool welcome

The euro's discreet entrance into the life of Parisians on January 1, 1999, might have gone unnoticed had it not been for extensive media coverage. Since then prices in stores and restaurants are quoted in euros and francs, while handy instant converters are readily available. However, until the franc is officially withdrawn on January 1, 2002, the euro remains low on a list of priorities of most French people.

PARIS IN FIGURES

City Growth
- 1851: Paris represented 3% of the French population
- 1921: Paris population was 3 million
- 1925: Exposition des Arts Décoratifs drew 16 million visitors
- 1954: Paris represented 15% of the population
- 1962–90: The number of foreigners in Paris doubled from 8% to 16%
- 1990: Only 22% of Parisians lived in central Paris (1st to 10th *arrondissement*)

People
- 10% of Parisians regularly attend mass
- 45% of Parisians go to the movies at least once a week
- Parisians, forming 4% of the population, provide 45% of total income-tax revenue
- 53% of Parisians use a car daily, 35% use public transportation
- 1.2 billion passengers travel by Métro every year
- 15% of Parisians are manual workers
- 30% of Parisians are executives or intellectuals
- 300,000 students attend Paris University
- 20 million tourists visit Paris annually
- 45% of Parisians live alone
- 90% of French women and 50% of French men use perfume

Population
- 2.1 million inhabitants within the city walls (decreasing last population census, 1990)
- 10.6 million inhabitants in the Île de France (increasing last population census, 1990)
- 52,000 inhabitants per square mile and an average of 1.92 per residence

Life
- The Paris region has 49 hospitals (24 in Paris alone) with a capacity of 40,000 beds
- The 1980s per capita cultural budget for Paris was 20 times that of the provinces
- The Louvre had 6.3 million visitors in 1994
- 200,000 Parisian dogs produce 11 tons of excrement daily
- 40% of street trees are plane trees
- There are 15,000 restaurants, cafés and clubs
- During July and August over 2 million cars join the holiday exodus

PARIS PEOPLE

PIERRE GAGNAIRE

Since Joël Robuchon, France's top chef for almost two decades, retired in 1996, a new star has risen on the Parisian gastronomic scene. Pierre Gagnaire left a three-star restaurant in Saint-Étienne to open a new one just off the Champs Élysées in 1997 and in less than a year he was rewarded with the ultimate Michelin consecration of three stars.

JEAN-PAUL GAULTIER

Now in his mid-40s, Jean-Paul Gaultier is still a prime mover in the fickle French fashion world. After spending his formative years with *haute-couturiers* Pierre Cardin and Jean Patou, in 1979 he created his own label. From his first "James Bond" collection, through "Dadism," "Witches," and "High-Tech," Gaultier aimed to shock. Costumes for films, mobile furniture, a record, and TV shows in the UK have paralleled his two annual fashion collections.

Jean-Paul Gaultier

PHILIPPE STARCK

A tripod orange-squeezer, chairs with pointed legs, a laughing TV—these are the hallmarks of Starck's design success. A "Made in France" phenomenon of the 1980s, Starck—gregarious, corpulent, and bearded—has presence in the 1990s. Still going strong is his redesign of the nightclub Les Bains Douches, while his latest gimmick is a mail-order house-kit composed of plans, a videotape, and a hammer.

WOMEN IN THE LIMELIGHT

Chic TV interviewer Anne Sinclair, who hit the limelight with her charm and sharp intellect, abandoned her popular program, *7 sur 7*, in 1997 when her husband became finance minister. Not before she had set a trend though: controversial minister of labor and social affairs Martine Aubry's strong personality and feminine inflexibility command the admiration of her political opponents, while cool, efficient, sexy television newsreaders and interviewers like Claire Chazal and Carole Gaessler overshadow their male counterparts.

Jacques Chirac

For over 18 years Jacques Chirac, the ebullient mayor of Paris and leader of the Gaullist party (RPR), surveyed the city from his palatial working residence overlooking the Seine, the Hôtel de Ville, and relaxed by reading Chinese poetry (in French). He transformed the city's infrastructure and repeatedly clashed with the ruling Socialists until in May 1995, after two previously unsuccessful attempts, he was finally elected president of France.

9

A Chronology

c. 200 BC	Celtic tribe of Parisii settles on Île de la Cité.
c. AD 100	Growth of the Roman city of Lutetia, later Paris.
451	Ste Geneviève saves Paris from Attila the Hun.
1100s	Tragic love affair of Abélard and Héloïse.
1163	The rebuilding of Notre Dame starts.
1215	University of Paris founded.
1358	Royal family installed in Marais and Louvre.
1337–1453	Hundred Years War between France and England.
1430	Henry VI of England crowned king of France in Notre Dame.
1437	Charles VII regains control of Paris.
1572	St Bartholomew's Massacre ignites Wars of Religion.
1600s	Paris reorganized; Le Marais developed.
1648–52	Civil uprising of La Fronde.
1671	Louis XIV moves to Versailles.
1700s	Development of Faubourg Saint-Germain.
1789	Storming of the Bastille; National Assembly makes Declaration of the Rights of Man.
1792	Monarchy abolished; proclamation of the Republic.
1793–94	Reign of Terror; Louis XVI beheaded. Inauguration of the Musée du Louvre.
1804	Napoleon Bonaparte crowned emperor.
1800–14	Building of imperial monuments. Founding of Grandes Écoles; increased centralization.

1830	Bourbons overthrown; Louis-Philippe crowned.
1848	Revolution topples Louis-Philippe; Second Republic headed by Napoleon III.
1852–70	Baron Haussmann transforms urban Paris.
1870–71	Paris besieged by Prussians, civil uprising of the Commune, Republic restored.
1889	Eiffel Tower built for Exposition Universelle.
1900	Grand and Petit Palais built for Exposition Universelle; first Métro line opens.
c. 1908	Cubism born in Montmartre with Picasso.
1914–18	Paris bombarded by German cannon, Big Bertha.
1925	Exposition des Arts Décoratifs introduces art-deco style.
1940	Nazis occupy Paris.
1944	Liberation of Paris led by Général Leclerc.
1954	National funeral for writer Colette.
1958	De Gaulle called in to head Fifth Republic.
1969	Les Halles market transferred to Rungis.
1977	Jacques Chirac elected first mayor of Paris since 1871. Centre Georges Pompidou opens.
1981	Election of President Mitterrand initiates *Grands Projets*.
1989	Bicentennial celebrations of the Revolution.
1995	Election of President Chirac.
1996	Bibliothèque Nationale François Mitterrand opened at Tolbiac.
1998	France wins soccer World Cup as host nation.

11

PEOPLE & EVENTS FROM HISTORY

*Napoleon Bonaparte
(1769–1821)*

REVOLUTION

The Revolution of 1789 signaled the end of absolute royal power and the rise of popular democracy. The royal family was forced from Versailles to the Tuileries palace, but in 1792 this in turn was attacked and Louis XVI and Marie-Antoinette were imprisoned and sent to the guillotine. The years 1792–93 marked the high point of the Terror that was led by Robespierre, himself guillotined in 1794.

NAPOLEON

Napoleon Bonaparte's meteoric rise and fall from power (1800–14) left an indelible mark on the capital. Ambitious reforms included the construction of neoclassical buildings, while his military campaigns made Paris capital of the greatest European empire since Charlemagne. More important was the increased concentration of the nation's culture and government in Paris, something that decentralization has still not eradicated two centuries later.

OCCUPATION

The scars left by France's Vichy régime were most evident in Paris, occupied by the Nazis from 1940. Luxury hotels and public buildings were requisitioned, and communists and Jews were deported in their thousands. After the Allies landed in Normandy in June 1944, a week-long insurrection by Parisians opened a path for them into the capital. General Von Cholitz capitulated after disobeying Hitler's orders to blow up the city, and Paris was reborn.

"LE GÉNÉRAL"

De Gaulle's role as one of France's major 20th-century figures started during the Occupation, when he headed the Free French Forces from London, continued with the Liberation, and was consolidated when he was called from retirement to solve the divisive Algerian War and head the Fifth Republic in 1958. His rule heralded increased presidential powers, a burgeoning consumer society, and the prominence of France within the European Community.

Henri IV

Authoritarian, complex, and charismatic, Henri IV (1553–1610) was also Paris's first urban designer. In 1594, after renouncing Protestantism and uttering the legendary words "Paris is well worth a mass," he triumphantly entered the city as a long-needed unifying force. He instigated the building of Place Royale (Place des Vosges), Place Dauphine and the Pont Neuf, the rise of Le Marais, and the planting of 20,000 trees in the Tuileries before losing his life to an assassin's knife.

12

PARIS
how to organize your time

ITINERARIES   14–15
Latin Quarter
Stately Paris
Green Paris
Smart Shopping

WALKS   16–17
*Le Marais to the Place
   des Vosges*
*Place des Vosges to the
   Latin Quarter*

EVENING STROLLS   18
The Seine
Bastille

SIGHTSEEING TOURS   19

EXCURSIONS   20–21
Versailles
Vaux-le-Vicomte
Giverny

WHAT'S ON   22

ITINERARIES

One of the pleasures of Paris is its compact scale and efficient public transportation. Visiting monuments in the central *arrondissements* is easiest and
most scenic on foot, and always includes obligatory café stops, but do not
hesitate to dive into the Métro for a short trip to more distant sights.

ITINERARY ONE	LATIN QUARTER
Morning	Climb the tower of Notre Dame (➤ 43) for a bird's-eye view over the city. Walk by the river to the Sainte Chapelle (➤ 39). Cross to boulevard Saint-Michel and walk up to the Musée de Cluny (➤ 38). Continue up boulevard Saint-Michel to the Jardin du Luxembourg (➤ 37).
Lunch	Have lunch in a café near the Panthéon.
Afternoon	Walk to Église Saint-Étienne-du-Mont (➤ 52). Explore the winding streets to the rue Monge. Look at the Roman Arènes de Lutèce (➤ 59). Walk south toward the Mosquée (➤ 52) and indulge in a mint tea. Visit the Jardin des Plantes botanical garden and Muséum National d'Histoire Naturelle (➤ 51).
ITINERARY TWO	STATELY PARIS
Morning	Cross Pont Neuf (➤ 55) to the island and take a boat trip along the Seine that returns to the island. Wander along the *quai* at river level to the Musée d'Orsay (➤ 31).
Lunch	Have lunch at the Musée d'Orsay, or walk up rue de Bellechasse and across boulevard Saint-Germain to the Musée Rodin (➤ 29), with its rose-garden café.
Afternoon	Continue to Les Invalides (➤ 28) and visit the Église du Dôme (➤ 28). Walk along the esplanade to cross the ornate Pont Alexandre III (➤ 55). Visit the Petit Palais (➤ 27) and explore the Champs Élysées (➤ 27). Catch bus No. 42 down avenue Montaigne to the Eiffel Tower (➤ 26). If it is getting late, this is an ideal place to view the sunset.

ITINERARY THREE	**GREEN PARIS**
Morning	Start the day at the Musée Marmottan (► 24), then take the Métro to Franklin D. Roosevelt. Walk down the paths of the Champs Élysées (► 27) to place de la Concorde (► 30). Cross over and walk through the Tuileries (► 56), stopping for a drink at a kiosk or along the terrasse du Bord de l'Eau for lovely views of the Left Bank.
Lunch	Have lunch at the Café Marly (► 53) or in the Louvre's subterranean labyrinth.
Afternoon	Visit a section of the Louvre's immense collection (► 35), then recover in the gardens of the Palais Royal (► 59). Take bus No. 67 from the rue du Louvre to Pigalle, where you can catch the Monmartrobus to the top of Montmartre hill. The views from Sacré Cœur (► 33) are superb.
ITINERARY FOUR	**SMART SHOPPING**
Morning	Start from Havre-Caumartin Métro station. Explore the department stores along boulevard Haussmann. At Chausseé d'Antin, turn right past the Opéra Garnier (► 32) then right again. The famous Café de la Paix (► 53) is on the corner. Walk toward place de la Madeleine; on the left is the Galerie des Trois Quartiers, an elegant shopping center.
Lunch	Walk round Paris's most famous delicatessens, Fauchon and Hédiard, or eat a cheese lunch at the Ferme-Saint-Hubert at 21 rue Vignon nearby.
Afternoon	Admire the luxury shops along rue Royale, turn left onto rue Saint-Honoré then left again to place Vendôme, the center of the jewelry trade. Take rue Danielle-Casanova on the right and then continue straight on past Galeries Vivienne and Colbert (► 36) to place des Victoires lined with fashion boutiques.
Evening	Dine at Au Pied de Cochon in rue Coquillière. 15

WALKS

THE SIGHTS

- Porte de Clisson
- Les Enfants Rouges
- Cathédrale Sainte-Croix-de-Paris
- Musée Picasso (➤ 51)
- Hôtel de Chatillon
- Musée Carnavalet (➤ 46)
- Place des Vosges (➤ 47)

INFORMATION

Distance 2 miles
Time 1–2 hours
Start point Plateau Beaubourg
🚇 H5–H6
🚍 Rambuteau, Hôtel de Ville
End point Place des Vosges
🚇 J6
🍴 Café Beaubourg, rue Saint-Martin; Ma Bourgogne, Place des Vosges (➤ 70)

Mère et enfant, Picasso

LE MARAIS TO THE PLACE DES VOSGES

After breakfast at the Café Beaubourg walk behind the Centre Georges Pompidou and turn right onto the rue Rambuteau, a colorful food-shopping street. Turn left up the rue des Archives, with the magnificent turreted Porte de Clisson (1375) rising from the Hôtel de Soubise (1709) on your right. Continue past a monumental fountain (1624) on your left and the Hôtel Guénégaud (1650)—that houses the Musée de la Chasse—diagonally opposite. Keep walking straight on to the rue de Bretagne, where you can rest in the leafy Square du Temple or investigate the leather-clothes market in the Carreau du Temple. Have a coffee nearby.

Along the rue de Bretagne, enter the picturesque food and flower market of Les Enfants Rouges (dating from the 1620s), then exit onto the rue Charlot. Walk south past the impressive Cathédrale Sainte-Croix-de-Paris, a former 17th-century convent, to the rue des Quatre-Fils. Turn left, past a new building that houses the National Archives, and continue to the rue Vieille-du-Temple. Circle round the garden of the Hôtel Salé, now home to the Musée Picasso, then continue to the Parc-Royal, where a small garden is overlooked by a row of superbly restored 17th-century mansions. Take a look at the courtyard of the Hôtel de Chatillon at 13 rue Payenne, then continue to rue de Sévigné. Admire the two mansions of the Musée Carnavalet, then continue across to the picturesque place du Marché Sainte-Catherine. Turn left onto rue Saint-Antoine and left again to the place des Vosges where you can stop to have lunch at Ma Bourgogne.

PLACE DES VOSGES TO THE LATIN QUARTER

Walk through a passageway at No. 9 place des Vosges to the courtyard of the Hôtel de Sully. Exit onto the rue Saint-Antoine, turn right and cross to rue Saint-Paul, lined with antique shops. Farther down on the right enter the Village Saint-Paul, a discreetly situated bric-a-brac market, then emerge on the other side into the rue des Jardins Saint-Paul. Here you see the largest remaining section of Philippe-Auguste's city wall. Turn left, then right along the rue de l'Ave Maria to reach the Hôtel de Sens, an exceptional example of 15th-century Gothic architecture. Look at the courtyard and the small formal garden behind the mansion. From here cross the Pont Marie to the Île Saint-Louis, turn right and walk along the quai de Bourbon and the quai d'Orléans, admiring the 17th-century mansions and the view of Notre Dame across the Pont Saint-Louis. Cross the Pont de la Tournelle to the Left Bank and end your day in the web of the Latin Quarter across the Seine.

THE SIGHTS

- Place des Vosges
- Village Saint-Paul (➤ 77)
- Philippe-Auguste's city wall
- Hôtel de Sens
- Île Saint-Louis (➤ 44)
- Institut du Monde Arabe (➤ 45)

INFORMATION

Distance 1 mile
Time 1–2 hours
Start point Place des Vosges
🚇 J6
🚇 Bastille, Chemin Vert, Saint-Paul
End point Latin Quarter, around boulevard Saint-Michel, rue Saint-Jacques
🚇 G6–H6; G7–H7

Place des Vosges   17

EVENING STROLLS

The Conciergerie at the Palais de Justice

THE SEINE

Start at Châtelet and walk toward the Louvre along the embankment opposite the illuminated Conciergerie, the Monnaie (Mint), and the Institut de France. At the Louvre make a detour into the Cour Carrée, magnificently lit and often deserted at night. Return to the river, cross the lively Pont des Arts, then walk back along the opposite bank, this time with views north of the stately Samaritaine and the Palais de Justice on the Île de la Cité. Continue toward Saint-Michel, then cross over to Notre Dame and make your way around the north side of the island, which offers views of the Île Saint-Louis, the Hôtel de Ville and the Gothic Tour Saint-Jacques towering over the place du Châtelet.

BASTILLE

From the place de la Bastille walk up the rue de la Roquette until the road forks. Turn right along the bustling pedestrian street of rue de Lappe that is packed with bars, nightclubs, and restaurants. (Keep an eye out for No. 71, a fine 18th-century house). Then turn left onto the rue de Charonne. Pass art galleries and more bars before cutting back to the rue de la Roquette via the rue Keller. Turn left and Notre-Dame de l'Espérance looms on your right, and at No. 68 there is a fountain (1839). Back at the fork turn right along rue Daval and cross two boulevards to rue du Pas de la Mule that then leads to the place des Vosges.

SIGHTSEEING TOURS

WALKING AND BUS TOURS

CAISSE DES MONUMENTS HISTORIQUES ET DES SITES
Daily program of walking tours with lecturers.
✉ 62 rue Saint-Antoine 75004   ☎ 01 44 61 21 69   🚇 Bastille, Saint-Paul   💷 Moderate

The Ville de Paris (municipality) offers guided tours to the Parc de Bagatelle, the Parc André Citroën, and the Père Lachaise, Montmartre, and Passy cemeteries.
☎ 01 40 71 75 60

BALABUS
Public bus service with stops, between Gare de Lyon and La Grande Arche de la Défense.
☎ 08 36 68 41 14   🕐 Apr–Sep: Sun 12:30PM–8:30PM; journey time 1 hour 15 minutes   🚇 Gare de Lyon/Grande Arche   💷 Whole trip: 3 Métro tickets or Paris-Visite/Mobilis travel passes

BOAT TRIPS

BATEAUX PARISIENS TOUR EIFFEL
✉ Rive Gauche, Port de la Bourdonnais   ☎ 01 44 11 33 44
🕐 Mon–Thu 10AM–10:30PM; Fri, Sat 10AM–11PM; every 30 min   🚇 Trocadéro   💷 Moderate

BATEAUX VEDETTES DU PONT-NEUF
Classic hour-long trip along the Seine.
✉ Square du Vert Galant 75001   ☎ 01 53 00 98 38   🕐 Daily 10AM–11PM   🚇 Pont Neuf   💷 Moderate

BATOBUS
Riverboat shuttle service; six stops between the Eiffel Tower and the Hôtel de Ville.
✉ Port de la Bourdonnais   ☎ 01 44 11 33 99   🕐 Daily 10–7 every 25 min   🚇 Trocadéro   💷 One and two-day passes, moderate

CANAUXRAMA
Three-hour canal trip between the Bastille and the Bassin de la Villette; reservation essential.
✉ Bassin de la Villette, 13 Quai de la Loire 75019   ☎ 01 42 39 15 00   🕐 Departures at 9:30 and 2:45 from Bassin de la Villette; 9:45 and 2:30 from the Port de l'Arsenal, Bastille   🚇 Jaurès or Bastille   💷 Expensive

Paris's canals

Cruising Paris's canals offers a more idiosyncratic view of Paris than the usual Seine trip. The revamped Arsenal dock at the Bastille (1806) is the kickoff for an underground vaulted passage that re-emerges at the Canal Saint-Martin. Chestnut trees, swing bridges, locks, the Hôtel du Nord (of movie fame), and modern apartment blocks lead to the Bassin de la Villette with its famous Rotonde (built by Ledoux in 1789). From here the Canal de l'Ourcq continues to the Parc de la Villette and then on eastwards for a further 67 miles.

EXCURSIONS

INFORMATION

Versailles

✉ Château de Versailles

☎ 01 30 84 76 18

◉ State apartments May–Sep: Tue–Sun 9–6:30. Oct–Apr: Tue–Sun 9–5:30. Grand and Petit Trianon May–Sep: Tue–Fri 10–12:30, 2–6:30; Sat, Sun 10–6:30. Oct–Apr: close 5:30. Park daily 7AM–sunset. Fountains May–Sep: Sun 3:30–5

🍴 Cafés, restaurants

🚊 RER Line C Versailles Rive Gauche

♿ Few

🎫 Château: expensive. Park: free

❓ Guided tours

Vaux-le-Vicomte

✉ Château de Vaux-le-Vicomte, 77950 Maincy

☎ 01 64 14 41 90

◉ Mid-Mar to mid-Nov: daily 10–6. Fountains Apr–Oct: second and last Sat of month 3–6. Candlelit tours May to mid-Oct: Thu, Sat 8PM–midnight

🍴 Restaurant

🚊 SNCF Gare de Lyon to Melun, then taxi

♿ Few

🎫 Moderate

❓ Self-guided audio tours

Giverny

✉ Fondation Claude Monet, 27620 Giverny

☎ 01 32 51 28 21

◉ Apr–Oct: Tue–Sun 10–6

🍴 Restaurant

🚊 SNCF Gare Saint-Lazare to Vernon, then bus, rent a bike or walk (3½ miles)

♿ Good

🎫 Expensive

CHÂTEAU AND PARK OF VERSAILLES

Few tourists fail to visit Versailles, the ultimate symbol of French grandeur and sophistication, and the backdrop to the death throes of the monarchy. In 1661, when Louis XIV announced his intention of moving his court to this deserted swamp, it was to create a royal residence, seat of government, and home to French nobility. Building continued until his death in 1715, by which time the 250-acre park had been tamed to perfection by Le Nôtre. Hundreds of statues, follies and fountains, and the royal love nests of the Grand and Petit Trianon relieve the formal symmetry, while rowboats, bicycles, and a minitrain now offer a diversion from history. Inside the château, visit the Grands Appartements (the official court and entertainment halls) that include the staggeringly ornate Hall of Mirrors with painted ceilings by Lebrun. The Petits Appartements (the royal living quarters) display France's most priceless examples of 18th-century decoration and may be visited by guided tour only.

The Latona fountain, Versailles

VAUX-LE-VICOMTE

About 30 miles southeast of Paris lies the inspiration for Versailles, a château erected in 1656 by Louis XIV's ambitious regent and minister of finance, Nicolas Fouquet, who employed France's most talented artists and craftsmen. Five years later, a château-warming party of

The lily pond at Giverny

extravagant proportions provoked Louis XIV's envy and resulted in the arrest and imprisonment of Fouquet for embezzlement. Today, the interior and magnificent grounds have been entirely restored and include the Musée des Équipages (horse-drawn carriages) in the stables. Inside the château, resplendent with Lebrun's painted ceilings, do not miss the rich Chambre du Roi. In front of the château's neo-classical facade stretch terraces, lawns, fountains, and statues, these ending at a canal. If you have time, continue your stroll in the woods beyond.

GIVERNY

This small Normandy village is famous for one reason—Claude Monet. The painter lived in the village from 1883 until his death in 1926, inspiring a local artists' colony and producing some of Impressionism's most famous and startling canvases. His carefully tended garden with its Japanese-style lily pond gradually became his sole inspiration, and was as important to him as his painting. Only reproductions of his works are displayed here, but the colorfully painted house, his personal collection of Japanese prints, and the beautiful garden together offer a wonderful day out. May and June, when the borders are a riot of color, is the best time for the flowers.

Le Petit Trianon

The Petit Trianon, the jewel in the crown of French neoclassical architecture, was built for Louis XV's mistress, Madame du Barry, and later presented by Louis XVI to his wife, Marie-Antoinette (who was to utter the inept words "let them eat cake" from her royal chambers as the angry mob below clamored for bread). In a pursuit of the simple life, Marie-Antoinette transformed the grounds into a "wild" park, complete with a make-believe village where she tended sheep.

21

WHAT'S ON

Information on current events is best found in *Pariscope*, an inexpensive weekly listings magazine (out on Wednesday) that covers everything from concerts to cinema, theater, sports, and nightclubs; it has a useful section in English. *Figaroscope* comes with *Le Figaro* on Wednesdays and also offers a good round-up of current events.

January	*America Stakes* at Vincennes racetrack.
February	*National Rugby Tournament.*
April	*International Paris Fair*: Stands promote gastronomy, tourism, and publications from all over the world.
	Paris Marathon.
May	*Labor Day* (May 1): Endless processions, thousands of bouquets of symbolic lilies of the valley, and no newspapers.
	Armistice Day (May 8).
June	*Festival Foire Saint-Germain*: Village traditions revived in Saint-Germain-des-Prés.
	Fête de la Musique (midsummer's night): Crowds spring to life during this government-sponsored event that schedules major rock and world-music bands.
	Course des Garçons de Café (late June): Over 500 waiters and waitresses career along the streets, each armed with tray, bottle, and glasses.
July	*Bastille Day* (July 14): Number one on the French festival calendar—celebrates the 1789 storming of the Bastille. Fireworks and street dances take over on the evening of July 13, while the 14th itself is devoted to a military parade on the Champs Élysées.
August	Annual exodus and *Fête des quartiers*: Outdoor concerts and street theater.
September	*Festival d'Automne à Paris* (mid-September until the end of December): Music, theater, and dance performances throughout the city.
October	*Foire Internationale d'Art Contemporain*: Paris's biggest modern art fair, at the Pavillon du Parc, Paris Expo, Porte de Versailles.
November	*Beaujolais Nouveau* (third Thursday in November): Liberal amounts of wine are drunk when the first bottles hit Paris.
	Antiques fair at Pelouse d'Auteuil, place de la Porte de Passy.
December	*Paris International Boat Show* at the Porte de Versailles.

PARIS's
top 25 sights

The sights are shown on the maps on the inside front cover and inside back cover, numbered **1–25** from west to east across the city

1 *Musée Marmottan*   *24*
2 *Palais de Chaillot*   *25*
3 *Tour Eiffel*   *26*
4 *Champs Élysées &* *Arc de Triomphe*   *27*
5 *Les Invalides*   *28*
6 *Musée Rodin*   *29*
7 *Place de la Concorde*   *30*
8 *Musée d'Orsay*   *31*
9 *Opéra de Paris*   *32*
10 *Sacré Cœur*   *33*
11 *Musée des Arts Décoratifs* *34*
12 *Musée du Louvre*   *35*
13 *Galeries Vivienne &* *Colbert*   *36*
14 *Jardin du Luxembourg* *37*
15 *Musée de Cluny*   *38*
16 *Sainte Chapelle*   *39*
17 *Conciergerie*   *40*
18 *Centre Georges Pompidou* *41*
19 *Marché aux Puces de* *Saint-Ouen*   *42*

20 *Notre Dame*   *43*
21 *Île Saint-Louis*   *44*
22 *Institut du Monde Arabe* *45*
23 *Musée Carnavalet*   *46*
24 *Place des Vosges*   *47*
25 *Cimetière du Père Lachaise* *48*

MUSÉE MARMOTTAN

HIGHLIGHTS

- *Impression—soleil levant,* Monet
- *Bouquet de Fleurs,* Gauguin
- Gold table-tray
- Geographical clock
- *Promenade près d'Argenteuil,* Monet
- *Charing Cross Bridge,* Monet
- *L'Allée des Rosiers,* Monet
- *Le Pont Japonais,* Monet
- Monet's *Water-Lilies* series
- Monet's spectacles

INFORMATION

- B6
- 2 rue Louis-Boilly 75016
- 01 42 24 07 02
- Tue–Sun 10–5:30
- La Muette
- 32
- RER Line C Boulainvilliers
- Moderate
- Bois de Boulogne (➤ 56)

One of the few incentives to get out into the residential 16th arrondissement is the Marmottan, where a mesmerizing collection of Monet paintings makes for a colorful escape from the urban aspects of the Parisian landscape.

Rich donations This often overlooked treasure of Parisian culture offers an eclectic collection built up over the years from the original donation of Renaissance and First Empire paintings and furniture given to the nation by the art historian Paul Marmottan in 1932. His discreetly elegant 19th-century mansion, furnished with Renaissance tapestries and sculptures and Napoleonic furniture, was later given an extra boost by the stunning Wildenstein collection of 230 illustrated manuscripts from the 13th to the 16th centuries, as well as an exceptional donation from Michel Monet that included 65 works by his father Claude Monet, the Impressionist painter. Works by Monet's contemporaries Gauguin, Renoir, Pissarro, Sisley, Berthe Morisot, and Gustave Caillebotte add to the Impressionist focus, but it is above all Monet's luminous canvases of dappled irises, wisteria, and water-lilies, dating from his last years at Giverny, that are memorable.

Shame It happens even to the best of museums, but when nine major paintings were stolen from the Marmottan in 1985 it caused acute embarrassment, not least because the booty included Monet's seminal work, *Impression—soleil levant*, that gave the art movement its name. Five years later, after a police operation on a worldwide scale, the plundered paintings were discovered in Corsica. They are now on display once again, needless to say under greatly increased security.

Top: Impression—soleil levant, *Monet*

PALAIS DE CHAILLOT

With its majestic wings curving toward the Eiffel Tower across the Seine, and its monumental presence, the Palais de Chaillot impresses. But it also has a human aspect: roller-skating heroes, mime artists, and Sunday promenaders.

Attractions The 1937 Exposition Universelle instigated the Palais de Chaillot's columns, these punctuated with bronze statues that overlook terraces and fountains. This spectacular art-deco wrapping contains three museums, a theater, and the Cinémathèque Française. The west wing houses the Musée de l'Homme and the Musée de la Marine, the former catering to anthropology and the latter to maritime and naval interests. A newly converted gallery at the Musée de l'Homme houses temporary thematic exhibitions, while the main collection gathers dust upstairs awaiting imminent renovation. On the top floor is the Salon de la Musique that displays some 500 "world" musical instruments used for Sunday concerts.

An exhibit in the maritime museum

Fire The building's east wing was damaged by fire in 1997 and its two museums are now closed. The Musée du Cinéma will find a new home in the Maison du Cinéma that is due to open in 2001 in the former American Center; as for the Musée des Monuments Français, conceived by Viollet-le-Duc to illustrate French architecture from prehistory to the 19th century, it is due to reopen in 2002 as part of the Cité de l'architecture et du patrimoine devoted to the national heritage and contemporary architecture.

HIGHLIGHTS

- Napoleon's imperial barge
- *Ports de France*, Vernet
- *Le Valmy*
- Contemporary French navy
- African frescoes
- Javanese *gamelan* orchestra
- King Béhanzin

INFORMATION

- ✚ D5
- ✉ Place du Trocadéro 75016
- ☎ Marine: 01 53 65 69 69
  Homme: 01 44 05 72 72
- 🕐 Marine: Wed–Mon 10–6.
  Homme: Wed–Mon
  9:45–5:15
- 🍴 Le Totem restaurant in the west wing
- Ⓜ Trocadéro
- 🚌 22, 30, 32, 63
- ♿ Few
- 💷 Moderate
- ↔ Musée d'Art Moderne de la Ville de Paris (➤ 50)
- ❓ Guided tours of Marine on request; ethnological films at Homme Wed and Sat 3PM, 4PM; Sun 3PM

TOUR EIFFEL

HIGHLIGHTS

- Panoramic views
- Bust of Gustave Eiffel

DID YOU KNOW?

- Weight: over 7,700 tons
- Made of 15,000 iron sections
- Height: 1,050 feet
- Top platform at 906 feet
- 1,652 steps to the top
- 55 tons of paint needed to repaint it
- 370 suicides

INFORMATION

- ✚ D6
- ✉ Champ de Mars 75007
- ☎ 01 44 11 23 23
- 🕐 Sep–Jun: daily 9:30AM–11PM. Jul–Aug: daily 9AM–midnight
- 🍴 Altitude 95 (2nd floor ☎ 01 45 55 20 04), Jules Verne (3rd floor ☎ 01 45 55 61 44)
- Ⓜ Bir-Hakeim
- 🚌 42, 82
- 🚈 RER Line C, Tour Eiffel
- ♿ Very good (to 3rd floor)
- 💵 Expensive; stairs cheap
- ↪ Les Invalides (➤ 28)

The Eiffel Tower could be a cliché but it isn't. The powerful silhouette of Gustave Eiffel's marvel of engineering still makes a stirring sight, especially at night when its delicate, lace-like iron structure comes to the fore.

Glittering feat Built in a record two years for the 1889 Exposition Universelle, the controversial Eiffel Tower was never intended to be a permanent feature of the city. However, in 1910 it was finally saved for posterity, so preparing the way for today's 4 million annual visitors. Avoid long lines for the elevator by visiting the tower at night, when it fully lives up to its romantic image and provides a glittering spectacle—whether the 292,000-watt illumination of the "staircase to infinity" itself, or the carpet of nocturnal Paris unfolding at its feet.

Violent reactions Gustave Eiffel was a master of cast-iron structures, his prolific output including hundreds of factories, churches, railroad viaducts, and bridges on four continents. His 1,050-foot tower attracted great opposition, but his genius was vindicated by the fact that it sways no more

than 5 inches in high winds and remained the world's highest structure for 40 years. Eiffel kept an office here until his death in 1923; from it he may have seen Comte de Lambert circle above in a flying-machine in 1909, or a modern-day Icarus plummet to his death from the parapet in 1912.

4

CHAMPS ÉLYSÉES & ARC DE TRIOMPHE

You may not be enamored of fast-food outlets and airline offices, both of which are major features of this once-glamorous avenue. But a recent face-lift has upgraded it, and nothing can change the magnificent east–west perspective.

Slow start It was Marie de Médicis, wife of Henri IV, who first made this a fashionable boulevard in 1616, but it was the celebrated landscape designer André Le Nôtre who contributed to its name—Elysian Fields—by planting alleys of trees and gardens. The heyday came in 1824 when new sidewalks and fountains made it the most fashionable prom-enading spot in Paris, with cafés and restaurants catering to a well-heeled clientele. The crown-ing glory was the Arc de Triomphe (►57), commissioned by Napoleon, while the 1900 Exposition Universelle added the glass and iron domes of the Grand Palais (which includes the Palais de la Découverte) and the Petit Palais at the lower end.

Parades Despite being dominated by commer-cial and tourist facilities, the Champs Élysées remains the symbolic focal point for national ceremonies, whether the traditional July 14 mil-itary parade, Armistice Day's wreath-laying at the Arc de Triomphe, or the fast-pedaling *grande finale* of the Tour de France. On the occasion of the 1989 Bicentennial celebrations, Jessye Norman led a spectacular host of swaying performers down to the place de la Concorde.

Luxury These days the Champs Élysées may be dominated by automobile showrooms, but plush film theaters, upscale stores, and one or two fashionable watering holes still remain to tempt those who want to see and be seen.

HIGHLIGHTS

- Arc de Triomphe
- Rude's *Marseillaise* sculpture on Arc de Triomphe
- L'Étoile
- Bluebell Girls at Lido
- Fouquets restaurant
- Palais de l'Élysée
- Ledoyen restaurant
- Grand Palais
- Petit Palais
- Philatelists' market

INFORMATION

- D4–E4; E5–F5
- Champs Élysées 75008
- Grand Palais: 01 44 13 17 17. Petit Palais: 01 42 65 12 73. Découverte: 01 40 74 80 00
- Grand Palais: Wed–Mon 10–8. Petit Palais: Tue–Sun 10–5:40. Palais de la Découverte: Tue–Sat 9:30–6; Sun 10–7
- Grand Palais: average cafeteria. Cafés and restaurants on Champs Élysées
- Charles de Gaulle-Étoile, Georges V, Franklin-D. Roosevelt, Champs-Élysées-Clémenceau
- 32, 42, 73
- Good
- Moderate to expensive
- Place de la Concorde (►30)
- Photo library and scientific films in Palais de la Découverte

27

LES INVALIDES

HIGHLIGHTS

- 643-foot facade
- Sword and armor of François I
- Salle Orientale
- Napoleon's stuffed horse
- *Emperor Napoleon*, Ingres
- Galerie des Plans-Reliefs
- Napoleon's tomb
- Église du Dôme
- 17th-century organ
- A Renault light tank

INFORMATION

- ✚ E6
- ✉ Esplanade des Invalides 75007
- ☎ Musée de l'Armée: 01 44 42 37 72
- 🕐 Oct–Mar: daily 10–5. Apr–Sep: daily 10–6. Napoleon's tomb: mid-Jun to mid-Sep 10–7
- 🚇 La Tour Maubourg, Invalides, Varenne
- 🚌 28, 49, 69, 93
- 🚆 RER Line C Invalides
- ♿ Good
- 💰 Moderate
- ↔ Musée Rodin (➤ 29)
- ❓ Guided tours on request ☎ 01 44 42 37 72; films on World Wars I and II

The gilded dome rising above the Hôtel des Invalides recalls the pomp and glory of France's two greatest promoters— the Sun King, who built Les Invalides, and the power-hungry Napoleon Bonaparte, who is entombed there.

Glory The vast, imposing edifice of Les Invalides was built to house invalid soldiers, and it continues to accommodate a few today. Its classical facade and majestic Cour d'Honneur date from the 1670s, with the ornate Église du Dôme completed in 1706 and the long grassy esplanade established soon after. The home of military institutions, Les Invalides is also a memorial to the succession of battles and campaigns that have marked French history and which are illustrated in the Musée de l'Armée. Here you can trace the evolution of warfare from early days to World War II, and there are daily screenings of war films.

The Cour d'Honneur

Tombs There are more relics inside the Église Saint-Louis, where tattered enemy standards hang despondently from cornices, but it is above all the baroque cupolas, arches, columns, and sculptures of the Église du Dôme that highlight France's military achievements and heroes. Tombs of generals fill the chapels while the crypt contains Napoleon's grandiose sarcophagus (which incorporates six successive layers), guarded by 12 statues, symbols of his military campaigns.

MUSÉE RODIN

As a complete antidote to the military might of Les Invalides, wander into the enchanting Musée Rodin, often forgotten by Parisians. This surprisingly peaceful enclave lifts you out of the hurly-burly of the boulevards into another sphere.

Hard times This rococo mansion, built for a prosperous wig-maker in 1730, has a checkered history. One owner (Maréchal de Biron) was sent to the guillotine, and the house has been used successively as a dance hall, convent, school, and as artists' studios. Rodin lived here from 1908 until his death in 1917, with such neighbors as the poet Rainer Maria Rilke and dancer Isadora Duncan. In 1919 the house was transformed into a museum.

Sculpture The elegant, luminous interior houses the collection of works that Rodin left to the nation on his death in 1917. It ranges from his early academic sketches to the later watercolors, and displays many of his most celebrated white marble and bronze sculptures, including *The Kiss*. There are busts of the composer Mahler, the suffragette Eva Fairfax, and Victor Hugo to name but a few, as well as a series of studies of Balzac in paunchy splendor. Alongside the Rodins are works by his contemporaries, in particular his tragic mistress and model, Camille Claudel, as well as Eugène Carrière, Munch, Renoir, Monet, and van Gogh. Rodin's furniture and antiques complete this exceptional collection.

Retreat The museum's private gardens are Paris's third largest and contain several major sculptures, a pond, flowering shrubs, benches for a quiet read, a converted chapel used for temporary exhibitions, and an open-air café.

HIGHLIGHTS

- *Les Bourgeois de Calais*
- *Le Penseur*
- *La Porte de l'Enfer*
- *Le Baiser*
- *La Main de Dieu*
- *Saint Jean Baptiste*
- *Adam et Eve*
- *Ugolin*
- *Le Père Tanguy*, van Gogh
- *Original staircase*

INFORMATION

➕ F6
✉ 77 rue de Varenne 75007
☎ 01 47 05 01 34
🕐 Oct–Mar: Tue–Sun 9:30–4:45. Apr–Sep: Tue–Sun 9:30–5:45
🍴 Peaceful garden café
Ⓠ Varenne
🚌 69
♿ Good
✋ Inexpensive
↔ Les Invalides (➤ 28)

7

PLACE DE LA CONCORDE

HIGHLIGHTS

- Jeu de Paume
- Hieroglyphs
- Hôtel Crillon
- *Chevaux de Marly*
- View up the Champs Élysées

DID YOU KNOW?

- The Egyptian obelisk weighs 250 tons
- 133 people were trampled to death here in 1770
- 1,300 heads were guillotined here in 1793–95

INFORMATION

- ✚ F5
- ✉ Place de la Concorde 75008
- ☎ Jeu de Paume: 01 42 60 69 69
- 🕐 Jeu de Paume: Wed–Fri noon–7; Tue noon–9:30; Sat, Sun 10–7
- 🍴 Small café in Jeu de Paume
- Ⓜ Concorde
- 🚌 24, 42, 52, 72, 73, 84, 94
- ♿ Jeu de Paume: excellent
- 💷 Moderate to expensive
- ↔ Champs Élysées & Arc de Triomphe (➤ 27), Jardin des Tuileries (➤ 56)

As you stand in this noisy traffic-choked square it is hard to imagine the crowds baying for the deaths of Marie-Antoinette and Louis XVI, who were both guillotined here at the height of the Terror of the French Revolution.

Chop-chop This pulsating square was initially laid out in 1775 to accommodate a statue of King Louis XV. Under the new name of place de la Révolution it then witnessed the mass executions of the French Revolution, and was finally renamed the place de la Concorde in 1795 as revolutionary zeal abated. In the 19th century, Guillaume Coustou's *Chevaux de Marly* were erected at the base of the Champs Élysées (those you see today are reproductions, the originals now housed in the Louvre). Crowning the center of the Concorde is a 3,000-year-old Egyptian obelisk overlooking eight symbolic statues of French cities. Use the pedestrian crossing to reach the central island and get a closer look at the obelisk framed by two romantic fountains.

Grandeur To the north, bordering the rue Royale, stand the colonnaded Hôtel Crillon (on the left) and the matching Hôtel de la Marine (right), both relics from pre-Revolution days. The rue Royale itself, with its luxury establishments, leads to the Madeleine. The eastern side of the Concorde is dominated by two public art galleries: the Jeu de Paume (by rue de Rivoli), that displays contemporary art exhibitions; and the Orangerie (nearer the river), famous for its impressive basement panels of Monet's *Water Lilies* (closed for refurbishing until August 2001). Visible across the bridge to the south is the Palais Bourbon, home to the Assemblée Nationale (French parliament).

8

MUSÉE D'ORSAY

You'll either love or hate the conversion of this turn-of-the-century train station, but whatever your view its art collections, covering the years from 1848 to 1914, are a must for anyone interested in the output of this crucial period.

Monolithic When this museum finally opened in 1986 controversy ran high: Gae Aulenti's heavy stone structures lay unhappily under Laloux's delicate iron and glass shell, built as a train terminus in 1900. But the collections redeem this *faux pas*, offering a solid overview of the momentous period from Romanticism to Fauvism. Ignore the monolithic mezzanine blocks and, after exploring the 19th-century

paintings, sculptures, and decorative arts on the first floor, take the escalator to the upper level. Here the Pont-Aven and Impressionist schools are displayed along with the giants of French art—Degas, Monet, Cézanne, van Gogh, Renoir, Sisley, and Pissaro. And don't miss the views from

The Church at Auvers, *van Gogh*

the outside terrace and café behind the station clock at the top.

To the ball The middle level is devoted to painting (Symbolism, Naturalism, and the Nabis) and sculpture from 1870 to 1914, and includes works by Rodin, Bourdelle, and Maillol. In the spectacular ballroom hang paintings by Gérôme and Bouguereau.

HIGHLIGHTS

- *Olympia*, Manet
- *Déjeuner sur l'Herbe*, Manet
- *Orphée*, Gustave Moreau
- *La Mère*, Whistler
- *L'Angélus du Soir*, Millet
- *La Cathédrale de Rouen*, Monet
- *L'Absinthe*, Degas
- *La Chambre à Arles*, van Gogh
- *Femmes de Tahiti*, Gauguin
- Chair by Charles Rennie Mackintosh

INFORMATION

- ✚ F6
- ✉ 1 rue de Bellechasse 75007
- ☎ 01 40 49 48 14; 01 40 49 48 48
- 🕐 Tue–Sat 10–6; Sun 9–6; Thu 10–9:45
- 🍴 Café des Hauteurs for good snacks; plush restaurant/ tea room on middle level
- Ⓜ Solférino
- 🚌 24, 68, 69
- Ⓡ RER Line C Musée d'Orsay
- ♿ Excellent
- 🅿 Moderate
- ↔ Musée du Louvre (➤ 35)
- ❓ Self-guided audio and guided tours, concerts, and lectures

OPÉRA DE PARIS

HIGHLIGHTS

- Grand Escalier
- Grand Foyer
- *Apollo*, Millet
- Facade
- Lamp-bearers

DID YOU KNOW?

- Garnier's design was selected from 171 others
- The total surface area of the building is 118,400 sq feet
- The auditorium holds 2,200 spectators
- The stage accommodates over 450 performers

INFORMATION

- ✚ G4
- ✉ Place de l'Opéra 75009
- ☎ Monument, museum and tours: 01 40 01 22 63 recorded information updated daily. Bookings: 01 44 73 13 00. Museum: 01 47 42 07 02
- 🕐 Daily 10–4:30
- 🍴 Bar open during shows
- Ⓜ Opéra
- 🚌 20, 21, 22, 27, 29, 42, 52, 53, 66, 68, 81, 95
- 🚆 RER Auber
- ♿ Few, call for appointment
- 💰 Moderate
- ↔ Place de la Concorde (► 30)
- ❓ Guided tours daily year round; in English Aug: ☎ 01 40 01 22 63

This is an ornate wedding cake of a building, but the sumptuous and riotous details that decorate its every surface are in fact the perfect epitaph to the frenetic architectural activities of the Second Empire.

Past glory When Charles Garnier's opera house was inaugurated in 1875 it marked the end of Haussmann's ambitious urban face-lift and announced the sociocultural movement to the belle-époque, with Nijinsky and Diaghilev's Ballets Russes as later highlights. Today the Salle Garnier mostly stages dance with only some opera, many prestigious operatic performances having been switched to the Opéra Bastille when the latter opened in 1989. Rudolf Nureyev was director of the Paris Ballet here between 1983 and 1989, and this was where he first danced in the West. Nureyev was succeeded by Patrick Dupond whose brilliant career prompted him to leave the Opéra in 1998. He was followed by Brigitte Lefèvre.

Dazzle Competing with a series of provocative lamp-bearing statues, the Palais Garnier's extravagant facade of arches, winged horses, friezes, and columns is topped by a verdigris dome and leads into a majestic foyer. This is dominated by the Grand Escalier, dripping with balconies and chandeliers, in turn sweeping upward to the Grand Foyer and its gilded mirrors, marble, murals, and Murano glass. Do not miss the equally ornate auditorium, with its dazzling gold-leaf decorations and red-velvet seats, and Marc Chagall's incongruous false ceiling, painted in 1964. The Opéra is open outside rehearsals (best bet is 1–2PM); enter through Riccardo Pedruzzi's 1990s library and the museum of operatic memorabilia.

SACRÉ CŒUR

Few people would admit it, but the high point of a trip up here is not the basilica itself but the stunning views. You can't forget, however, that Sacré Cœur was built in honor of the 58,000 dead of the Franco-Prussian War.

Weighty Although construction started in 1875, it was not until 1914 that this white neo-Romanesque-Byzantine edifice was completed, partly due to the problems of laying foundations in the quarry-riddled hill of Montmartre. Priests still work in relays to maintain the tradition of perpetual prayer for forgiveness of the horrors of war and for the massacre of some 20,000 Communards by government troops. The

square bell tower was an afterthought and houses one of the world's heaviest bells, La Savoyarde, that weighs in at 21 tons. The stained-glass windows are replacements of those that were shattered by enemy bombs in 1944.

Byzantine mosaic of Christ, chancel vault

Panoramas This unmistakable feature of the Paris skyline magnetizes the crowds arriving either by funicular or via the steep steps of the terraced garden. Dawn and dusk offer sparkling panoramas over the city, especially from the exterior terrace of the dome, the second-highest point in Paris after the Eiffel Tower (access is from the left-hand side of the basilica). Just to the east of Sacré Cœur is the diminutive Saint Pierre, a much reworked though charming church that is all that remains of the Benedictine abbey of Montmartre founded in 1133.

HIGHLIGHTS

- La Savoyarde bell
- View from the dome
- Mosaic of Christ
- Treasure of Sacré Cœur
- Bronze doors at Saint Pierre
- Stained-glass gallery
- Statue of Christ
- Statue of Virgin Mary and Child
- The funicular ride from Abbesses Métro station

INFORMATION

- ✚ H3
- ✉ 35 rue Chevalier de la Barre 75018
- ☎ 01 53 41 89 00
- 🕐 Basilica: daily 7AM–11PM. Dome and crypt Apr–Sep: daily 9–7. Oct–Mar: daily 9–6
- 🚇 Abbesses, then funicular
- 🚌 Montmartrobus from Pigalle or Abbesses
- ♿ Few
- 🎫 Basilica: free. Dome and crypt: cheap
- ↔ Montmartre Village (rue Lepic, Vineyard of Montmartre, place des Abbesses)

MUSÉE DES ARTS DÉCORATIFS

HIGHLIGHTS

- 13th-century Italian painting
- Sculpted wood and stone altarpieces
- Decorative panels from Cremona, Italy
- 16th-century inlaid wood paneling
- Italian majolica
- Renaissance bronzes
- Venetian glass
- 15th-century furniture
- Late-medieval bedroom

INFORMATION

- G5
- 107 rue de Rivoli 75001
- 01 44 55 57 50
- Tue–Fri 11–6; Sat, Sun 10–6; late night Wed 9PM
- Palais-Royal/Musée du Louvre
- 21, 27, 39, 48, 67, 69, 72, 81
- Excellent
- Moderate
- Musée du Louvre (➤ 35)

The discreet old-fashioned atmosphere of this fascinating museum devoted to interior design and decoration was blown away by President Mitterrand's **grand projet** *that swept right through the Louvre palace.*

Looking back The Musée des Arts Décoratifs is one of four museums forming the Union Centrale des Arts Décoratifs founded at the end of the 19th century by a group of industrialists and collectors wishing to exhibit "Beauty in function." Throughout the 20th century contributions by designers such as Le Corbusier, Mallet-Stevens, Nikki de Saint Phalle, and Philippe Starck greatly enriched the collections. Extensive renovation of the museum, housed since 1905 in the Marsan wing of the Louvre, is underway; meantime, the medieval and Renaissance department reopened in 1998.

Medieval and Renaissance Department The exotic collections, spanning the 13th to the 16th century, are displayed with stunning effect in nine rooms where religious paintings, sculptures and furniture contrast with exquisite objects of daily life. The Galerie des Retables contains remarkable examples of altarpieces in carved wood or stone from all over Europe. One room is named after the Maître de la Madeleine, a 13th-century Italian painter, whose *Virgin and Child between St Andrew and St James* is proudly displayed among other works ranging from the primitive to the late Gothic style. The Salle des Vitraux has beautiful 16th-century stained glass, while a selection of tapestries is exhibited in rotation in the Salle des Tapisseries. The 17th- to 20th-century collections will be on display again in 2001 but special exhibitions continue to be organized in the meantime.

Top: A richly decorated 16th-century carpet from India

MUSÉE DU LOUVRE

Nocturnal lighting transforms the Louvre's glass pyramid entrance into a gigantic cut diamond—just a foretaste of the treasures contained within. It is hard to ignore the state-of-the-art renovation, but that is just the icing on the cake.

The world's largest museum Few visitors bypass this palatial museum, but definitions of personal interest need to be made beforehand as mere wandering can become a long and unrewarding occupation. Since 1981 the Louvre has been undergoing a radical transformation that crowns six centuries of eventful existence and is due to be completed in 2000. Originally a medieval castle, it first took shape as an art gallery under

François I, eager to display his Italian loot. Catherine de Médicis transformed it into a palace in 1578. After escaping the excesses of the revolutionary mob, in 1793 it became a people's museum and was later enlarged by Napoleon I, who also greatly enriched its collection.

Mona Lisa, Leonardo da Vinci

Art fortress The vast collection of some 30,000 exhibits is arranged on four floors of three wings: Sully (east), Richelieu (north), and Denon (south), while beneath the elegant Cour Carrée lie the keep and dungeons of the original medieval fortress. Do not miss the two spectacular skylit halls flanking the passageway from Palais Royal that display monumental French sculptures, nor the tasteful shops in the central marble hall.

HIGHLIGHTS

- Palace of Khorsabad
- Glass pyramid entrance, designed by I. M. Pei
- *Bataille de San Romano,* Uccello
- *Mona Lisa,* da Vinci
- *La Dentellière,* Vermeer
- *Vénus de Milo*
- Cour Carrée at night

INFORMATION

- G5–G6
- 99 rue de Rivoli 75001
- 01 40 20 53 17. Recorded information in 5 languages: 01 40 20 51 51, Auditorium: 01 40 20 51 86
- Thu–Sun 9–6; Mon and Wed 9AM–9:45PM
- Wide selection of restaurants and cafés
- Palais-Royal/Musée du Louvre
- 21, 27, 39, 48,67, 68, 69, 72, 74, 75, 76, 81, 85, 95
- Excellent
- Very expensive until 3PM, moderate after 3PM and Sun
- Musée des Arts Décoratifs (➤ 34), Musée d'Orsay (➤ 31)
- Guided and digital tours; regular lectures, films, workshops, concerts in auditorium
  To avoid long lines, buy your ticket in advance
  08 03 80 88 03
  or via the Internet: www.louvre.fr

GALERIES VIVIENNE & COLBERT

HIGHLIGHTS

- Mosaic floor
- Bronze statue
- Staircase at 13 Galerie Vivienne
- Clock
- Bookstore

DID YOU KNOW?

- Explorer Bougainville lived here
- Revolutionary Simón Bolivar lived here
- Crook-turned-cop Vidocq lived here in the 1840s

INFORMATION

- ✚ G5
- ✉ Galerie Vivienne & Galerie Colbert 75002
- ◷ Gate at 5 rue de la Banque is permanently open
- 🍴 Le Grand Colbert (➤ 73)
- Ⓜ Bourse, Palais-Royal/ Musée du Louvre
- 🚌 29
- ♿ Good
- 🎟 Free
- ↔ Jardin du Palais-Royal (➤ 59)

The mosaic floor (top) and the bronze statue (right) in the Galerie Vivienne

These connecting 19th-century passages, with their original mosaic floors and neo-classical decoration, are a perfect place for people-watching, and they offer a complete contrast to the fashionable buzz of neighboring streets.

Shopping arcades Between the late 18th and early 19th centuries the Right Bank included a network of 140 covered passageways—the fashionable shopping malls of the time. Today there are fewer than 30, of which the Galeries Vivienne and Colbert are perhaps the best known, squeezed in between the Bibliothèque Nationale and the place des Victoires. Bookworms and fashion-victims cross paths in this elegant, skylit setting lined with potted palms, where there is also the occasional fashion show. It is perfect for a rainy day browse.

Hive of interest The Galerie Vivienne (1823) opens onto three different streets, while the parallel Galerie Colbert (1826) has its own entrances. Colbert is now an annex of the Bibliothèque Nationale, and regular exhibitions (prints, photos, theater accessories) and concerts are held in its galleries and auditorium. Galerie Vivienne is commercial in spirit: this is where you can track down designer watches, antiquarian or rare artists' books (bookstore established in 1826 at Nos. 45 and 46), contemporary design, fine wines, intriguing toys, or just sit sipping tea beneath the skylight, watching the world go by.

JARDIN DU LUXEMBOURG

Despite the crowds, these gardens are serene in all weather and are the epitome of French landscaping. The occupants present an idealized image of an unhurried Parisian existence far from the daily truth of noise and traffic.

Layout Radiating from the large octagonal pond in front of the Palais du Luxembourg (now the Senate) are terraces, paths, and a wide tree-lined alley that leads down to the Observatory crossroads. Natural attractions include shady chestnuts, potted orange and palm trees, lawns, and even an experimental fruit garden and orchard, while fountains, tennis courts, bee-hives, a puppet theater, and children's playgrounds offer other distractions. Statues of the queens of France, artists, and writers are dotted about the terraces and avenues.

Park activities All year round joggers work off their *foie gras* on the circumference, and in summer sunbathers and bookworms settle into park chairs, card- and chess-playing retirees claim the shade in front of the palace, bands tune up at the bandstand near the boulevard Saint-Michel entrance, and children burn off energy on swings and donkey rides.

History The Palais du Luxembourg and surrounding garden were originally commissioned by Marie de Médicis, wife of Henri IV, in 1615, and designed to resemble her childhood Florentine home. The Allée de l'Observatoire and the English-style garden were added in the early 19th century. A petition signed by 12,000 Parisians luckily saved the garden from Haussmann's urban ambitions, and since then its formal charms have inspired countless literary and cinematic tributes.

HIGHLIGHTS

- Médicis fountain
- Cyclops, Acis, and Galateus sculptures
- Bandstand
- Statue of Delacroix
- Orange-tree conservatory
- Experimental fruit garden
- Beekeeping school
- Statues of queens of France

DID YOU KNOW?

- Isadora Duncan danced here
- Ernest Hemingway claimed to capture pigeons here for his supper

INFORMATION

- ✚ G7
- ✉ 15 rue de Vaugirard 75006
- ☎ Senate: 01 42 34 20 60
- 🕐 Apr–Oct: daily 7:30AM–9:30PM. Nov–Mar: daily 8:15–5 (times may vary slightly)
- 🍴 Open-air cafés, kiosk restaurant
- Ⓜ Luxembourg
- 🚌 21, 27, 38, 58, 82, 84, 85, 89
- 🚆 RER Line B Luxembourg
- ♿ Very good
- 🎟 Free
- ↔ Église Saint-Sulpice (► 52)

MUSÉE DE CLUNY

HIGHLIGHTS

- *La Dame à la Licorne* tapestries
- Gold altar frontal
- *Pilier des Nautes*
- Heads from Notre Dame
- Visigothic votive crown
- Italian processional cross
- Statue of Adam
- Stained glass
- Averbode altarpiece
- Abbot's Chapel

INFORMATION

- ✚ H7
- ✉ 6 place Paul-Painlevé 75006
- ☎ 01 53 73 78 00
- 🕐 Wed–Mon 9:15–5:45
- Ⓜ Cluny-La Sorbonne
- 🚌 21, 27, 38, 63, 85, 86, 87, 96
- Moderate
- ↔ Sainte Chapelle (➤ 39)
- ❓ Guided tours of vaults, baths, and collections: information and reservation
  ☎ 01 53 73 78 16

Take a deep breath outside the Musée de Cluny (officially the Musée National du Moyen-Age/Thermes de Cluny) and prepare to enter a time warp in which the days of the troubadours and courtly love are re-created in its paneled rooms.

Baths The late 2nd-century Roman baths adjoining the Hôtel de Cluny are composed of three stone chambers: the Caldarium (steam bath), the Tepidarium (tepid bath), and the Frigidarium (cold bath), with ruins of the former gymnasium visible on the boulevard Saint-Germain side. Important Roman stonework is exhibited in the niches, while Room VIII houses 21 mutilated heads from Notre Dame. Recent excavations have also opened up a labyrinth of Roman vaults that can be toured with a guide.

Treasures The Gothic turreted mansion was built in 1500 by the abbot Jacques d'Amboise and is one of France's finest examples of domestic architecture of this period. Some 23,000 objects compose the collection, much of which was gathered by the 19th-century medievalist and collector, Alexandre du Sommerard. Perhaps the most famous piece is the beautiful *La Dame à la Licorne* tapestry, woven in the late 15th century. Six enigmatic panels depict a woman, a lion and a unicorn, animals, flowers, and birds, all exquisitely worked. Costumes, accessories, textiles, and tapestries are of Byzantine, Coptic, or European origin, while the gold- and metalwork room houses some outstanding pieces of Gallic, Barbarian, Merovingian, and Visigothic artistry. Stained glass, table games, ceramics, wood carvings, illuminated manuscripts and Books of Hours, altarpieces, and religious statuary complete this exceptional and very manageable display.

Top: À mon Seul Désir, *one of the* La Dame à la Licorne *tapestries*

SAINTE CHAPELLE

Sainte Chapelle's 246-foot spire soaring towards the heavens is in itself an extraordinary expression of faith, but inside this is surpassed by the glowing intensity of the magnificent stained-glass windows reaching up to a star-studded roof.

Masterpiece One of Paris's oldest and most significant monuments stands within the precincts of the Palais de Justice. The chapel was built by Louis IX (later canonized) to house relics he had acquired at exorbitant cost during the crusades, and which included what was reputed to be the Crown of Thorns, as well as fragments of the

Cross and drops of Christ's blood (now kept in Notre Dame). Pierre de Montreuil masterminded this delicate Gothic construction, bypassing the use of flying buttresses, incorporating a lower chapel for palace servants and installing 6,650 square feet of stained glass above. Completed in 1248 in record time, it served as Louis IX's private chapel with discreet access from what was then the royal palace.

Apocalypse No fewer than 1,134 biblical scenes are illustrated in the 16 windows, starting with Genesis and finishing with the Apocalypse (the central rose window). To follow the narrative chronologically, read from left to right and bottom to top, row by row. The statues of the Apostles against the pillars are mostly copies—the damaged originals are at the Musée de Cluny.

HIGHLIGHTS

- Rose window
- Oratory
- 19th-century restoration
- Tombs of canons
- Stained glass depiction of Christ's Passion
- Saint Louis himself in the 15th window

INFORMATION

- ✚ H6
- ✉ 4 boulevard du Palais 75001
- ☎ 01 53 73 78 51
- 🕐 Oct–Mar. daily 10–5. Apr–Sep: daily 9:30–6:30
- Ⓜ Cité, Saint-Michel
- 🚌 21, 38, 85, 96
- 🚈 RER Line B, Saint-Michel
- 🚻 Moderate
- ↔ Musée de Cluny (▶ 38)

Top: the stained-glass windows of the upper chapel

CONCIERGERIE

HIGHLIGHTS

- Public clock
- Sculptures
- Marie-Antoinette's cell
- Tour Bonbec

DID YOU KNOW?

- 288 prisoners were massacred here in 1792
- 4,164 citizens were held here during the Terror
- Comte d'Armagnac was assassinated here
- 22 left-wing Girondins were held in one room
- Robespierre spent the night here before his execution
- There were three types of cell according to prisoners' means

INFORMATION

- H6
- 1 quai de l'Horloge 75001
- 01 53 73 78 50
- Oct–Mar: daily 10–4:30. Apr–Sep: daily 9:30–6
- Cité, Châtelet
- 21, 38, 47, 85, 96
- Moderate
- Sainte Chapelle (➤ 39)
- Guided tours: daily 11AM and 3PM

The ghosts of the victims of the guillotine must surely haunt this stark and gloomy place that served as a prison and torture chamber for over five centuries, and remains full of macabre mementos of its grisly past.

Gloom Rising over the Seine in menacing splendor, the turreted Conciergerie was built from 1299 to 1313 originally to house Philippe-le-Bel's caretaker (*concierge*) and palace guards, and with Sainte Chapelle it formed part of a royal complex on the Île de la Cité. The square, corner tower displays Paris's first public clock, an ornate masterpiece constructed in 1370 and restored along with the rest of the Gothic interior in the 19th century. Access to the Conciergerie is through the Salle des Gardes, a vaulted stone chamber now plunged into shadow by the embankment outside, that in turn opens onto the vast but equally gloomy Salle des Gens d'Armes. This is thought to be one of Europe's oldest-surviving medieval halls, and is where members of the royal household ate their meals. From here, a curious spiral staircase leads to the original kitchens.

Victims From 1391 until 1914 the building functioned as a prison and torture chamber, its reputation striking fear into the hearts of the population. A network of cells, both shared and private, lines the corridor (the rue de Paris) leading to the Galerie des Prisonniers, where lawyers, prisoners, and visitors once mingled. A staircase leads up to rooms relating the Conciergerie's bloody history (including a list of the guillotine's 2,278 victims); back downstairs are re-creations of the Chapelle des Girondins, and the cells occupied by Marie-Antoinette, Danton, and Robespierre.

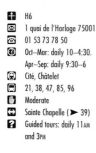

Top: Salle des Gens d'Armes

18

CENTRE GEORGES POMPIDOU

Late opening hours make an exhibition visit possible between an aperitif and dinner in this still-controversial cultural center. You can take your pick between the genesis of modernism, an art movie, or a drama performance.

High-tech culture More than a mere landmark in the extensive face-lift that Paris has undergone in the last 30 years, the high-tech Centre Pompidou (commonly known as Beaubourg) is a hive of constantly changing cultural activity. Contemporary art, architecture, design, photography, theater, cinema, and dance are all represented, while the lofty structure itself offers exceptional views over central Paris. Take the transparent escalator tubes for a bird's-eye view of the piazza where musicians, street artists, and portraitists ply their trades to the teeming crowds.

The fountain in nearby place Igor Stravinsky

Face-lift From October 1997 to the eve of the millennium in December 1999, the center underwent major restructuring and refurbishment, remaining closed apart from temporary exhibitions in the Galerie Sud. In 2000, the collection of the Musée National d'Art Moderne will be displayed on the 3rd and 4th levels. The 5th floor will house temporary exhibitions and a cafeteria-restaurant. In the meantime, visit the reopened Atelier Brancusi on the piazza, or spend francs at the museum store housed in the temporary tepee in front of the center.

HIGHLIGHTS

- Design by Richard Rogers, Renzo Piano, and Jean-François Bodin
- Stravinsky fountain
- *The Deep*, Jackson Pollock
- *Phoque*, Brancusi
- *Le Magasin*, Ben
- *Bleu II*, Miró
- *Infiltration homogène*, Joseph Beuys
- Gouache cut-outs, Matisse
- *Improvisations*, Kandinsky

INFORMATION

- ✚ H5–H6
- ✉ Rue Rambuteau 75004
- ☎ 01 44 78 12 33. Information on daily events: 01 44 78 14 63
- ⏰ Tepee: Mon, Wed–Fri, Sun 12:30–6; Sat 2–6
- 🍴 Café Beaubourg nearby (► 53)
- Ⓜ Rambuteau, Hôtel de Ville
- 🚌 38, 47, 75
- 🚇 RER Line A B, Châtelet-Les Halles
- ♿ Excellent
- 💵 Tepee: free admission; Atelier Brancusi: inexpensive
- ↔ Musée National des Techniques (► 51)
- ❓ Frequent lectures, concerts, parallel activities, Atelier des Enfants

Marché aux Puces de Saint-Ouen

HIGHLIGHTS

- Marché Serpette: antiques, art deco, jewelry
- Marché Paul Bert: antiques, quality bric-a-brac
- Marché Jules Vallès: bric-a-brac, furniture, prints
- Marché Biron: reproduction furniture, objets d'art
- Marché Vernaison: antiques
- Marché Cambo: paintings, furniture
- Marché Malik: secondhand clothes, accessories, ethnic goods

INFORMATION

- G1
- Porte de Clignancourt
- Sat–Mon 7:30–7
- Cafés and restaurants on rue des Rosiers
- Porte de Clignancourt, Porte de Saint-Ouen
- 56, 60, 85, 95
- Good
- Free
- Sacré Cœur (➤ 33)
- Beware of pickpockets

A Sunday pastime favored by many locals is to look for bargains at the city's flea markets, of which the crème de la crème is still this one. Nowhere else will you find such a fascinating cross-section of Parisian society.

Duck and banter The approach from the Métro to this sprawling 75-acre market is uninspiring as it entails bypassing household goods, jeans, and shoe stands before ducking under the *Périphérique* overpass and finally entering the fray. Persevere and you may discover an antique gem, a fake, or a secondhand pilot's jacket. Everything and anything is displayed here but all commerce is carried on in the true bantering style of the *faubourgs*, a habit that dates from the late 19th century when the first junkmen moved in to offer their wares for sale.

Bargain Registered dealers are divided into ten official markets that interconnect through passageways bustling with crowds. Along the fringes are countless hopefuls who set up temporary stands to sell a mind-boggling range of goods from obsolete kitchenware to old jukeboxes and cheap junk. Although unashamedly a tourist trap, there is something for everyone here, but do go early—trading starts at 7:30AM. Bargaining is obligatory and prices are directly related to the weather: high on sunny, crowded days and low under cold, wet skies. Stop for lunch in one of the animated bistros along the rue des Rosiers or try the terrace of A. Picolo at 58 rue Jules-Vallès (☎ 01 40 11 11 19). On weekends as many as 150,000 bargain-hunters, tourists, and dealers can cram the passageways—avoid Sunday afternoons in particular, when the throng reaches claustrophobic proportions and pickpockets abound.

20

NOTRE DAME

"Spectacular" is the word that springs to mind when describing Paris's most extraordinary monument, with its 295-foot spire and some of the world's best-known flying buttresses. One of the finest views of the cathedral is from the quais to the east.

Evolution Construction started on this labor of faith in 1163 but it was not finished until 1345, making it range in style between Romanesque and Gothic. Since then the cathedral has suffered from pollution, politics, aesthetic trends, and religious change. Louis XV declared stained glass outmoded and replaced most of the rose windows with clear glass (the stained glass was later restored), Revolutionary anticlericalism toppled countless statues, and the spire was amputated in 1787. Not least, Viollet-le-Duc, the fervent 19th-century medievalist architect, was let loose on its restoration and made radical alterations.

Interior grandeur The gloomy stone interior contains numerous chapels, tombs, and statues, as well as the sacristy (south side of choir) where the treasure of Notre Dame is kept. Climb the towers—386 steps—for fantastic views and a closeup of the gargoyles. Look closely at the three asymmetrical sculpted portals on the facade: these once served as a Bible for illiterate worshippers. Finally, walk round the cathedral for a view of its extravagant flying buttresses.

HIGHLIGHTS

- South rose window
- Porte Rouge
- Portail du Cloître
- Sculptures of the Portal de Sainte Anne
- Treasure of Notre Dame
- Emmanuel bell
- 1730 organ
- *Pietà*, Coustou
- Statue of Notre-Dame de Paris
- Choir stalls

INFORMATION

- ✚ H6
- ✉ Place du Parvis Notre-Dame 75004
- ☎ 01 42 34 56 10.
  Crypt: 01 43 29 83 51
- ⏰ Cathedral: daily 8–7.
  Tower and crypt Oct–Mar: daily 10–4:30. Apr–Sep: daily 10–5:30.
  Treasure: daily 9:30–6
- 🚇 Cité, Saint-Michel
- 🚌 24, 47
- 🚆 RER Lines B and C, Saint-Michel
- ♿ Good
- 💰 Cathedral: free. Tower and crypt: moderate.
  Treasure: inexpensive
- ↔ Musée de Cluny (➤ 38), Île Saint-Louis (➤ 44)
- ❓ Organ recitals at 5:30PM on Sun

The southern aspect of Notre Dame, showing the south rose window (detail above)

ÎLE SAINT-LOUIS

HIGHLIGHTS

- Église Saint-Louis-en-l'Île
- Doorway of Hôtel de Chenizot and Hôtel Lambert, rue Saint-Louis-en-l'Île
- Hôtel Lambert
- Camille Claudel's home and studio, 19 quai de Bourbon
- Square Barye
- Brasserie de l'Île Saint-Louis
- Pont Marie
- High-water mark, 1 quai d'Anjou
- Berthillon, 31 rue Saint-Louis-en-l'Île

INFORMATION

- H6–H7, J6–J7
- Sunny terrace of La Brasserie de l'Île
- Pont Marie, Sully Morland
- 67, 86, 87
- Good
- Notre Dame (➤ 43)

Floating mid–Seine is this fascinating residential island, a living museum of 17th-century architecture and also a popular tourist haunt. Join the crowds and spot an illustrious resident, but above all indulge in the island's own ice cream.

History Once a marshy swamp, the Île Saint-Louis was transformed into an elegant residential area in the 17th century, when it was joined to the

Courtyard, quai de Bourbon

Île de la Cité. Today, six bridges link it to the Right Bank and the Left Bank, but nevertheless it still maintains a spirit of its own, and residents openly boast that its food stores are unsurpassable. Cutting across it lengthwise is rue Saint-Louis-en-l'Île, lined with upscale groceries, arts and craft shops, and restaurants, and also home to the Église Saint-Louis-en-l'Île, begun by Le Vau in 1664. The side streets here are mainly residential.

Hashish The Quai d'Anjou, on the northeast side, has a rich past. Former residents include the architect himself, Le Vau, at No. 3, Honoré Daumier (No. 9), Baudelaire, and Théophile Gautier who, at No. 17, animated his Club des Haschichins. Commemorative plaques to the famous pepper the facades of the island's harmonious townhouses, and the riverside paths offer quintessential Parisian views, romantic trysts, and summer sunbathing. Before leaving, make sure you try a Berthillon ice cream, reputedly the best in the world.

INSTITUT DU MONDE ARABE

It is difficult to miss this gleaming, ultra-contemporary building as you cross the Seine. Although some may find it limited, the museum's collection nevertheless offers a sleekly presented introduction to the brilliance of Islamic culture.

Arab inspiration Clean lines, aluminum walls, and glass are the hallmarks of Jean Nouvel's design for the Arab Institute, which was inaugurated in 1987 to foster cultural exchange between Islamic countries and the West. Innovative features include high-speed transparent elevators, a system of high-tech metal screens on the south elevation that filter light entering the institute and which were inspired by the *musharabia* (carved wooden screens) on traditional Arab buildings, and an enclosed courtyard achieved by splitting the building in two. The institute's facilities comprise a museum, library, exhibition halls, audiovisual facilities, and an elegant rooftop café boasting spectacular panoramas across the Seine.

Museum First take the elevator to the 9th floor for sweeping views across the Île Saint-Louis and northeastern Paris, then head down to the museum on the 7th floor. Here, finely crafted metalwork, ceramics, textiles, carpets, and calligraphy reflect the exceptional talents of Islamic civilization, although the collection remains small in relation to its ambitious setting. Temporary exhibitions are often of a high quality and cover both historical and contemporary themes in arts, crafts, and photography. There is an audiovisual center in the basement with thousands of slides, photographs, films, and sound recordings, and current news broadcasts from all over the Arab world are also available for viewing.

HIGHLIGHTS

- Light screens
- Astrolabes in museum
- Sculpted wood and ivory
- Head of sun god
- Rope and palm-fiber sandal
- Sultan Selim III's Koran
- Miniature of Emperor Aurengzeb
- Indian glass vase
- Egyptian child's tunic

INFORMATION

- ✚ J7
- ✉ 1 rue des Fossés Saint-Bernard 75005
- ☎ 01 40 51 38 38
- 🕐 Tue–Sun 10–6
- 🍴 Convivial snack bar open until midnight; tea room
- Ⓜ Jussieu, Cardinal Lemoine
- 🚌 24, 63, 67, 86, 87, 89
- ♿ Excellent
- 🎫 Moderate
- ↔ Île Saint-Louis (➤ 44), Arènes de Lutèce (➤ 59)
- ❓ Occasional Arab music, films, and plays

MUSÉE CARNAVALET

HIGHLIGHTS

- Statue of Louis XIV
- Facade sculptures on Hôtel Carnavalet
- Le Brun's ceiling painting
- *Destruction of the Bastille*, Hubert Robert
- Bastille prison keys
- Le Sueur's comic-strip
- Proust's bedroom
- Ballroom from Hôtel de Wendel
- Napoleon's picnic-case

INFORMATION

- ✛ J6
- ✉ 23 rue de Sévigné 75003
- ☎ 01 42 72 21 13
- 🕐 Tue–Sat 10–5:40
- Ⓜ Saint-Paul
- 🚍 29, 96
- ♿ Excellent
- 💰 Moderate
- ↔ Place des Vosges (➤ 47), Musée Picasso (➤ 51)
- ❓ Photography exhibitions

There is no better museum than this to plunge you into the history of Paris, and its renovated mansion setting is hard to beat. Period rooms, artifacts, documents, paintings, and objets d'art combine to guide you through the city's turbulent past.

Ornamental excess This captivating collection is displayed within two adjoining 16th- and 17th-century town houses. Entrance is through the superb courtyard of the Hôtel Carnavalet (1548), once home of the celebrated writer Madame de Sévigné. Here attention focuses on the Roman period, the Middle Ages, the Renaissance, and the heights of decorative excess reached under Louis XIV, Louis XV, and Louis XVI. Some of the richly painted and sculpted interiors are original to the building; others, such as the wood paneling from the Hôtel Colbert de Villacerf and Brunetti's *trompe-l'œil* staircase paintings, have been brought in.

Revolution to the present Next door, the well-renovated Hôtel Le Peletier de Saint-Fargeau (1690) exhibits some remarkable objects from the Revolution—a period when anything and everything was emblazoned with slogans—and continues with Napoleon I's reign, the Restoration, the Second Empire, the Commune, and finally the belle-époque. Illustrious figures such as Robespierre and Madame de Récamier come to life within their chronological context. The collection ends in the early 20th century with some remarkable reconstructions of interiors, and paintings by Utrillo, Signac, Marquet, and Foujita.

PLACE DES VOSGES

Paris's best-preserved square connects the quarters of the Marais and the Bastille. Visitors always marvel at its architectural unity and love to stroll under its arcades, now animated by outdoor restaurants and window-shoppers.

Place Royale Ever since the square was inaugurated in 1612 with a spectacular fireworks display, countless luminaries have chosen to live in the red-brick houses overlooking the central garden of plane trees. Before that, the square was the site of a royal palace, the Hôtel des Tournelles (1407), that was later abandoned and demolished by Catherine de Médicis in 1559 when her husband Henri II died in a tournament. The arcaded facades were commissioned by the enlightened Henri IV, who incorporated two royal pavilions at the center of the north and south sides of the square and named it "Place Royale."

Celebrities After the Revolution the square was renamed place des Vosges in honor of the first French district to pay its new taxes. The first example of planned development in the history of Paris, these 36 town houses (nine on each side and still intact after four centuries) with their steep-pitched roofs surround a formal garden laid out with gravel paths and fountains. The elegant symmetry of the houses has always attracted a string of celebrities. Princesses, official mistresses, Cardinal Richelieu, the Duc de Sully, Victor Hugo (his house is now a museum) and Théophile Gautier, and more recently the late painter Francis Bacon, Beaubourg's architect Richard Rogers, and former minister of culture, Jack Lang, have all lived here. Upscale shops and chic art galleries, with prices to match and ideal for window-shopping, line its arcades.

HIGHLIGHTS

- Pavillon du Roi
- Statue of Louis XIII
- No. 6, Maison Victor Hugo
- No. 21, residence of Cardinal Richelieu
- Archaeological finds at No. 18
- Door knockers
- *Trompe-l'œil* bricks
- Auvergne sausages at Ma Bourgogne restaurant

INFORMATION

- ✚ J6
- ✉ Place des Vosges 75004
- 🍴 Ma Bourgogne (➤ 73)
- 🚇 Bastille, Chemin Vert, Saint-Paul
- 🚌 29, 96
- ♿ Good
- 🎫 Free
- ↔ Hôtel de Sully (➤ 17), Musée Carnavalet (➤ 46)

CIMETIÈRE DU PÈRE LACHAISE

HIGHLIGHTS

- Oscar Wilde's tomb
- Edith Piaf's tomb
- Chopin's tomb
- Marcel Proust's tomb
- Mur des Fédérés
- Delacroix's tomb
- Tomb of Victor Hugo's family
- Baron Haussmann's tomb
- Molière's tomb
- Jim Morrison's tomb

INFORMATION

- ✚ L5–M5; L6–M6
- ✉ Boulevard de Ménilmontant 75020
- ☎ 01 43 70 70 33
- 🕐 Oct–Mar: Mon–Fri 8–5:30; Sat 8:30–5:30; Sun 9–5:30. Apr–Sep: Mon–Fri 8–6; Sat 8:30–6; Sun 9–6
- Ⓜ Père Lachaise
- 🚌 61, 69
- ♿ Excellent
- ✋ Free
- ❓ Guided tours (in English Jun–Sep)

If you think cemeteries are lugubrious then a visit to Père Lachaise may change your mind. A plethora of tomb designs, shady trees, and twisting paths combine to create a peaceful setting that has become a popular park.

Pilgrimage This landscaped hillside, up in the *faubourgs* of Ménilmontant, is now a favorite haunt for rock fans, Piaf fans, and lovers of poetry, literature, music, and history. Since its creation in 1803 this vast cemetery has seen hundreds of the famous and illustrious buried within its precincts, so that a walk around its labyrinthine expanse presents a microcosm of French sociocultural history. Pick up a plan at the entrance or the kiosk by the Métro, then set off on this Parisian path of the Holy Grail to track down your heroes.

Incumbents The cemetery was created in 1803 on land once owned by Louis XIV's confessor, Father La Chaise. It was the site of the Communards' tragic last stand in 1871, when the 147 survivors of a nightlong fight met their bloody end in front of a government firing-squad and were thrown into a communal grave, now commemorated by the Mur des Fédérés in the eastern corner. A somber reminder of the victims of World War II are the memorials to those who died in the Nazi concentration camps. Paths meander past striking funerary monuments and the graves of such well-known figures as the star-crossed medieval lovers Abélard and Héloïse, painters Delacroix and Modigliani, actress Sarah Bernhardt, composers Poulenc and Bizet, and writers Balzac and Colette. Crowds of rock fans throng round the tomb of Jim Morrison, singer with The Doors, whose death in Paris in 1971 is still a mystery.

PARIS's *best*

Museums & Galleries	50
Places of Worship	52
Cult Cafés & Salons de Thé	53
20th-Century Architecture	54
Bridges	55
Green Spaces	56
Views	57
Children's Activities	58
Free Attractions	59
Intriguing Streets	60

MUSEUMS & GALLERIES

Other museums

If you are hooked on the intimate atmosphere of one-man museums, then head for the former home/studio of sculptor Antoine Bourdelle, renovated in 1992 by top architect Christian de Portzamparc (⊠ 18 rue Antoine-Bourdelle 75014 🖐 Falguière). Other jewels include the Maison de Victor Hugo (➤ 47), the Musée Delacroix (➤ 60), the Musée Hébert (➤ 60), and the Maison de Balzac (47 rue Raynouard 75016 🖐 Passy).

Visit the Musée d'Art Moderne for modern and contemporary paintings and sculpture

See Top 25 Sights for
CENTRE GEORGES POMPIDOU ➤ 41
GALERIE DU JEU DE PAUME ➤ 30
MUSÉE DE L'ARMÉE ➤ 28
MUSÉE DES ARTS DÉCORATIFS ➤ 34
MUSÉE CARNAVALET ➤ 46
MUSÉE DE CLUNY ➤ 38
MUSÉE DE L'HOMME, MUSÉE DE LA MARINE ➤ 25
MUSÉE DU LOUVRE ➤ 35
MUSÉE MARMOTTAN ➤ 24
MUSÉE D'ORSAY ➤ 31
MUSÉE RODIN ➤ 29
PETIT PALAIS, GRAND PALAIS ➤ 27

CITÉ DES SCIENCES ET DE L'INDUSTRIE
Vast, enthralling display covering the Earth, the universe, life, communications, natural resources, technology, and industry. There are temporary exhibitions, a planetarium, a children's section, and a THX movie theater, La Géode (➤ 58).
🔲 L2 ⊠ 30 avenue Corentin Cariou 75019 🕾 01 40 05 80 00 🕔 Tue–Sat 10–6; Sun 10–7 🍴 Cafés in park 🖐 Porte de la Villette 🖐 Expensive

MAISON EUROPÉENNE DE LA PHOTOGRAPHIE
Stylish new center for contemporary photography, which has permanent displays, workshops, and a library, and stages dynamic temporary shows.
🔲 J6 ⊠ 5–7 rue de Fourcy 75004 🕾 01 44 78 75 00 🕔 Wed–Sun 11AM–8PM 🖐 Saint-Paul 🖐 Moderate

MUSÉE D'ART MODERNE DE LA VILLE DE PARIS
Dufy's mural *La Fée Electricité*, Matisse's *La Danse*, and a solid collection of the early moderns offer a parallel to exhibitions of contemporary avant-garde artists.
🔲 D5 ⊠ 11 avenue du Président-Wilson 75016 🕾 01 53 67 40 00 🕔 Tue–Fri 10–5:30; Sat, Sun 10–6:45 🍴 Cafeteria 🖐 Iéna, Alma-Marceau 🖐 Moderate

MUSÉE GUSTAVE MOREAU
This museum is dedicated solely to the Symbolist painter Gustave Moreau (1826-98), teacher of Matisse and Rouault, and is housed in his former home and studio. Evocative paintings,

watercolors, and drawings are on display.

🚇 G4 ✉ 14 rue de la Rochefoucauld 75009 ☎ 01 48 74 38 50 🕐 Thu–Sun 10–12:45, 2–5:15; Mon and Wed 11–5:15 🚇 Trinité 🖐 Inexpensive

MUSÉE NATIONAL DES ARTS D'AFRIQUE ET D'OCÉANIE
Fascinating artifacts from the Pacific, Africa, and Maghreb, through to Australian Aboriginal art. Sculptures, textiles, jewelry, and masks. Children love the aquariums, and the building (1931) is stunning.
🚇 M8 ✉ 293 avenue Daumesnil 75012 ☎ 01 44 74 84 80; 🕐 Wed–Mon 10–5:30 🚇 Porte Dorée 🖐 Moderate

MUSÉE NATIONAL DES TECHNIQUES
An eccentric museum where art meets science through antique clocks, vintage cars, optics, and mechanical toys. Reopened in November 1999 after renovation.
🚇 J5 ✉ 60 rue Réaumur 75003 ☎ 01 53 01 82 20/50 🕐 Inquire by phone 🚇 Arts et Métiers, Réaumur-Sébastopol 🖐 Moderate

MUSÉE DU PANTHÉON BOUDDHIQUE (GUIMET)
While the magnificent Musée Guimet remains closed for major restructuring until spring 2000, visit the annex to meditate on Japanese and Chinese Buddhas.
🚇 D5 ✉ 19 avenue d'léna 75116 ☎ 01 45 05 00 98 🕐 Wed–Mon 9:45–5:45 🚇 léna 🖐 Inexpensive

MUSÉE PICASSO
Massive collection of Picasso's paintings, sculptures, drawings, and ceramics in a beautifully renovated 17th-century mansion. The fixtures are by Diego Giacometti, and some of the works are by Picasso's contemporaries.
🚇 J6 ✉ Hôtel Salé, 5 rue de Thorigny 75003 ☎ 01 42 71 25 21 🕐 Wed–Mon 9:30–5:30 🚇 Chemin Vert 🚌 29 🖐 Moderate

MUSÉUM NATIONAL D'HISTOIRE NATURELLE
Spectacular displays of comparative anatomy, paleontology, and mineralogy. Interesting temporary exhibitions and botanic gardens (1635).
🚇 J8 ✉ 57 rue Cuvier 75005 ☎ 01 40 79 30 00 🕐 Wed–Mon 10–6; Thu 10–10. Grande Galerie de l'Evolution (Paleontology and Mineralogy): 10–5 🚇 Monge, Gare d'Austerlitz 🖐 Expensive; reduced in morning

Grand Nu au Fauteuil Rouge, *in the Musée Picasso*

Musée Picasso
The contents of the Musée Picasso—no fewer than 200 paintings, 158 sculptures, and 3,000 drawings—were acquired by France in lieu of inheritance tax. The process of evaluating Picasso's vast estate was no simple task as he had the annoying habit of leaving a château once the rooms were filled with his prodigious works. Eleven years of cataloging followed by legal wrangling with his heirs finally produced this superb selection, one-quarter of his collection.

PLACES OF WORSHIP

Saint-Étienne-du-Mont

See Top 25 Sights for
NOTRE DAME ➤ 43
SACRÉ CŒUR ➤ 33
SAINTE CHAPELLE ➤ 39

ÉGLISE SAINT-ÉTIENNE-DU-MONT
Dating from the 15th century, a bizarre combination of Gothic, Renaissance, and classical architecture. Unique timber screen arching over the nave.
✚ H7 ✉ place Sainte-Genevieve 75005 🚇 Cardinal Lemoine

ÉGLISE SAINT-EUSTACHE
Renaissance in detail and decoration but medieval in general design. Frequent organ recitals.
✚ H5 ✉ rue Rambuteau 75001 🚇 Les Halles

ÉGLISE SAINT-GERMAIN-DES-PRÉS
Paris's oldest abbey dates from the 10th century; it preserves 12th-century flying buttresses, an original tower, and the choir. Regular organ recitals.
✚ G6 ✉ place Saint-Germain-des-Prés 75006
🚇 Saint-Germain-des-Prés

ÉGLISE SAINT-MERRI
Superb example of Flamboyant Gothic though not completed until 1612. Renaissance stained glass, murals, impressive organ loft, and Paris's oldest church bell (1331). Concerts are held regularly.
✚ H6 ✉ 78 rue Saint-Martin 75003 🚇 Hôtel de Ville

ÉGLISE SAINT-SÉVERIN
Rebuilt from the 13th to the 16th centuries on the site of a 12th-century oratory. Inside is an impressive double ambulatory, palm-tree vaulting, and the Chapelle Mansart. Some stained glass originated at Saint-Germain-des-Prés (late 14th century).
✚ H6 ✉ 1 rue des Prêtres Saint-Séverin 75005 🚇 Saint-Michel

ÉGLISE SAINT-SULPICE
Construction started in 1646 and ended 134 years later, producing asymmetrical towers and very mixed styles. Note Delacroix's murals in the first chapel on the right, France's largest organ, and statues by Bouchardon.
✚ G7 ✉ place Saint-Sulpice 75006 🕐 7:30–7:30
🚇 Saint-Sulpice

LA MOSQUÉE
This startling Moorish construction (1926) has a richly decorated interior, patio, and arcaded garden. Relax in the hammam (see panel ➤ 85) or sip mint tea.
✚ J8 ✉ place du Puits-de-l'Ermite 75005 ☎ 01 45 35 97 33
🕐 Guided tours: Sat–Thu 9–12, 2–6 🍴 Tea room 🚇 Jussieu
💰 Inexpensive

Saint-Germain-des-Prés
The first church of Saint-Germain-des-Prés was erected in the 6th century in the middle of fields (*les prés*). From the 8th century the church was part of a Benedictine abbey but was destroyed by the Normans, after which the present church was built. The monastery was surrounded by a fortified wall and adjoined a bishop's palace, but this eventually made way for housing in the late 17th century.

Cult Cafés & Salons de Thé

LES DEUX MAGOTS
Some 25 whiskey brands, a good mix of tourists, and the literary shades of Simone de Beauvoir, Truman Capote, and Hemingway. Strategic spot for street artists.

⊞ G6   ✉ 6 place Saint-Germain-des-Prés 75006
☎ 01 45 48 55 25
◷ Daily 7:30AM–1:45AM
Ⓜ Saint-Germain-des-Prés

Les Deux Magots, in Place Saint-Germain-des-Prés

CAFÉ BEAUBOURG
Opposite the Pompidou Centre, a favorite with artists, critics, and book-reading poseurs. Discreet tables in spacious setting designed by Christian de Portzamparc.

⊞ H6   ✉ 100 rue Saint-Martin 75004   ☎ 01 48 87 63 96
◷ Daily 8AM–1AM; Sat till 2AM   Ⓜ Hôtel de Ville/Chatelet/Rambuteau

LA CLOSERIE DES LILAS
Hot spot of history's makers and shakers, including Lenin, Trotsky, Verlaine, and James Joyce.

⊞ G8   ✉ 171 boulevard du Montparnasse 75006   ☎ 01 40 51 34 50   ◷ Daily 11–11   Ⓜ Vavin, Raspail

CAFÉ DE FLORE
Haunted by ghosts of existentialists Sartre and de Beauvoir, who held court here during the Occupation. Wildly overpriced but great for people-watching.

⊞ G6   ✉ 172 boulevard Saint-Germain 75006   ☎ 01 45 48 55 26
◷ Daily 7AM–1:30AM   Ⓜ Saint-Germain-des-Prés

CAFÉ MARLY
The latest in fashionable watering holes. Elegance is assured by the setting overlooking the Louvre pyramid, and by Olivier Gagnère's intelligent decoration.

⊞ G5   ✉ Cour Napoléon, 93 rue de Rivoli 75001   ☎ 01 49 26 06 60   ◷ Daily 8AM–2AM   Ⓜ Palais-Royal, Musée du Louvre

AUX DÉLICES DE SCOTT
Once frequented by Clemenceau and Sarah Bernhardt, elegant café with fine cakes and pastries.

⊞ E3   ✉ 39 avenue de Villiers 75017   ☎ 01 47 63 71 36
◷ 8:30AM–6:30PM   Ⓜ Malesherbes

MARIAGE FRÈRES
Chic and expensive tea room upstairs. Over 460 teas from 20 countries. Original shop is at 30 rue du Bourg-Tibourg in the Marais.

⊞ G6   ✉ 13 rue des Grands-Augustins 75006   ☎ 01 40 51 82 50
◷ Daily noon–7. Closed Aug   Ⓜ Odéon

The croissant

As you sit over your morning *café au lait* eating a croissant, meditate on the origins of this quintessential French product. It was invented when Vienna was besieged by the Turks in 1683. A baker heard underground noises and informed the authorities, who found the enemy tunneling away into the city. The baker's reward was permission to produce pastries—so he created one in the form of the Islamic crescent.

20TH-CENTURY ARCHITECTURE

See Top 25 Sights for
CENTRE GEORGES POMPIDOU ➤ 41
INSTITUT DU MONDE ARABE ➤ 45

Grands projets

President Mitterrand was responsible for many of Paris's late-20th-century monuments. For over a decade cranes groaned as the state's *grands projets* emerged from their foundations. Intellectual criteria often came before functional considerations, and consequently not all monuments operate successfully. The Louvre renovation, topped by I. M. Pei's pyramid, is a notable exception.

The Grande Arche at La Défense

BIBLIOTHÈQUE DE FRANCE
Mitterrand's last pet *grand projet*. Dominique Perrault's symbolic design was dogged by technical and functional problems until it finally opened in early 1997.
➕ K8 ✉ 11 quai François-Mauriac ☎ 01 53 79 59 59
🕐 Tue–Sat 10–7; Sun 12–6 🚇 Quai de la Gare

CITÉ DE LA MUSIQUE
Finally completed in 1995 after 16 years of delays and political volte-face, with a monumental design in white stone by Christian de Portzamparc. Houses a music school, concert hall, and museum of music.
➕ L2 ✉ 221 avenue Jean-Jaurès ☎ Museum 01 44 84 44 84
🕐 Tue–Sun noon–6 🍴 Café 🚇 Porte de Pantin

LA GRANDE ARCHE
A marble window on the world designed by Otto Von Spreckelsen and completed for the 1989 Bicentennial. Take the exterior elevator for views along the city's historical La Défense–Arc de Triomphe–Louvre axis.
➕ Off map at A2 ✉ 1 Parvis de La Défense ☎ 01 49 07 27 57
🕐 Daily 10–7; ticket office closes one hour earlier 🚇 La Défense
🎟 Moderate

MAISON DU VERRE
Designed in art-deco style by Pierre Chareau in 1932. Astonishing use of glass.
➕ G6 ✉ 31 rue Saint-Guillaume 75006 🚇 Rue du Bac

NO. 26 RUE VAVIN
This striking, innovative building—designed by Henri Sauvage in 1912—is faced in blue and white ceramic and has stepped balconies.
➕ G7 ✉ 26 rue Vavin 75006 🚇 Vavin

PORTE DAUPHINE
The best remaining example (1902) of Hector Guimard's art-nouveau Métro entrances, with a glass canopy and writhing sculptural structures.
➕ C4 ✉ avenue Bugeaud 75016 🚇 Porte Dauphine

RUE MALLET-STEVENS
This tiny cul-de-sac houses major symbols of "cubist" architecture (1927) by Robert Mallet-Stevens. The stark, purist lines and volumes continue at Le Corbusier's nearby Villa Laroche (1923), now a foundation.
➕ B6 ✉ rue Mallet-Stevens, off rue du Dr-Blanche 75016
🚇 Jasmin

BRIDGES

PONT ALEXANDRE III
Paris's most ornate bridge, rich in gilded cupids and elaborate lamps. Built for the 1900 Exposition Universelle, and dedicated to the Franco-Russian alliance of 1892—the foundation stone was laid in 1896 by Tsar Nicolas II, Tsar Alexander III's son.
🔶 E5 🔘 Invalides

PONT DE L'ALMA
Originally built in 1856 to commemorate victory over the Russians in the Crimean War. Replaced in 1974, it crosses the road tunnel in which Princess Diana was killed in 1997—now a place of pilgrimage.
🔶 E5 🔘 Alma-Marceau

PONT DES ARTS
The pedestrian bridge of 1804 was replaced in 1985 by an iron structure of seven steel arches crossed by resonant wooden planks. It's a favorite spot for impromptu parties and street performances.
🔶 G6 🔘 Louvre-Rivoli

PONT DE BIR-HAKEIM
Paris's double-decker bridge (1903–1905) is best experienced by rattling over it in a Métro. Designed by Formigé, with steel columns in art-nouveau style.
🔶 D6 🔘 Bir-Hakeim, Passy

PONT MARIE
Named after the Île Saint-Louis property developer, first built in 1635. Once lined with four-story houses—some later partly destroyed by floods and others demolished in 1788. Rebuilt in 1850.
🔶 J6 🔘 Pont Marie

PONT NEUF
Built 1578–1604, Paris's oldest bridge ironically bears the name of "New Bridge." The innovative, houseless design was highly controversial at the time. In 1985 it was "wrapped" by site-artist Christo.
🔶 G6–H6 🔘 Pont Neuf

PONT ROYAL
Five classical arches join the Tuileries with the Faubourg Saint-Germain area. Built in 1689 by Gabriel to Mansart's design, it was once used for major Parisian festivities and fireworks.
🔶 G6 🔘 Palais-Royal, Musée du Louvre

36 bridges
The Paris motto *"Fluctuat nec mergitur"* ("It floats but it never sinks") did not always hold true. For centuries there were only two bridges, which linked the Île de la Cité north and south. Subsequent wooden bridges sank without trace after floods, fires, or riverboat collisions, so the construction of the stone Pont Neuf marked a real advance. The city's 36th bridge, Pont Charles de Gaulle, now spans the Seine between the Bibliothèque de France and Bercy.

Pont Alexandre III

GREEN SPACES

Parc Monceau

Parc de Bagatelle

On the west side of the Bois de Boulogne is the Parc de Bagatelle. Its mini-château, built in 1775, was sold in 1870 to Englishman Richard Wallace who added further pavilions and terraces. About 700 varieties of roses bloom here and its open-air restaurant offers a romantic, summer-evening setting (see panel ➤ 66).

Jardin des Serres d'Auteuil

Off the tourist beat, and with striking late 19th century tropical greenhouses. The terrace wall is adorned with sculpted masks from Rodin's studio (🞤 A7 ⊠ 3 avenue de la Porte d'Auteuil 17607 ☎ 01 40 71 76 07 🕒 Daily 10–5, 6 in summer 🚇 Porte d'Auteuil).

BOIS DE BOULOGNE
An area of 2,090 acres, 14 miles of paths, 35 miles of roads, 150,000 trees, and 300,000 bushes. Distractions from boating to clay-pigeon shooting and gastronomy.
🞤 A4–A6, B4–B6 🕒 Permanently open 🍴 Cafés, restaurants 🚇 Porte Dauphine, Porte d'Auteuil

JARDIN DES TUILERIES
Laid out in 1564, later radically formalized by Le Nôtre. Now replanted to match adjoining Louvre. Maillol's statues rest in the shade of chestnut trees.
🞤 F5–G5 ⊠ place de la Concorde 75001 🕒 Daily dawn–dusk 🍴 Open-air cafés 🚇 Tuileries 🎟 Free

PARC ANDRÉ-CITROËN
A cool futurist park divided into specialist gardens, landscaped in 1980s on site of former Citroën factory.
🞤 C8 ⊠ rue Balard, rue Leblanc 75015 ☎ 01 45 57 13 35 🕒 Oct–Mar: daily 8:30–8. Apr–Sep: daily 8:30AM–10PM 🚇 Balard

PARC MONCEAU
Classic park planted in 1783 by Thomas Blaikie by order of the Duc d'Orléans. Picturesque *faux* ruins, statues, and Ledoux's rotunda create timeless setting.
🞤 E3 ⊠ boulevard de Courcelles 75008 ☎ 01 43 18 70 70 🕒 Oct–Mar: daily 7AM–8PM. Apr–Sep: daily 7AM–10PM 🚇 Monceau

PARC MONTSOURIS
A Haussmann creation designed on English models, with copses and serpentine paths. Small lake with swans, waterfall, and grotto. Summer bandstand.
🞤 G10 ⊠ avenue Reille/boulevard Jourdan 75014 🕒 Oct–Mar: daily 8:30–6. Apr–Sep: daily 8:30AM–10PM 🍴 Restaurant 🚇 RER Line B Cité Universitaire 🎟 Free

VIEWS

> **Don't forget superlative panoramas from**
> **CENTRE GEORGES POMPIDOU ➤ 41**
> **LA GRANDE ARCHE ➤ 54**
> **INSTITUT DU MONDE ARABE ➤ 45**
> **NOTRE DAME ➤ 43**
> **SACRÉ CŒUR ➤ 33**
> **TOUR EIFFEL ➤ 26**

ARC DE TRIOMPHE
Situated at the hub of Haussmann's web of 12 avenues, and the ultimate symbol of Napoleon's military pretensions and might. Video projections.
🚩 D4 ✉ place de l'Etoile 75008 ☎ 01 55 37 73 77 🕑 Oct–Mar: daily 10AM–10:30PM. Apr–Sep: daily 9:30AM–11PM 🚇 Charles de Gaulle-Etoile 🦽 Moderate

LA GRANDE ROUE
Dizzy views of the Tuileries and Louvre from the Ferris wheel at the heart of the amusement park.
🚩 G5 ✉ rue de Rivoli 75001 🕑 Late Jun to late Aug: Sun–Fri noon–11:45; Sat noon–12:45AM 🚇 Tuileries 🦽 Moderate

LA SAMARITAINE
The 10th floor at Magasin 2 offers a spectacular close-up on the city's Left Bank monuments. Lunch in the open air on the 9th floor or dine in splendor at the 5th-floor restaurant, Toupary (☎ 01 40 41 29 29 🕑 Mon–Sat lunch from 11:45, dinner 7:30–11:30).
🚩 H6 ✉ rue de la Monnaie 75001 ☎ 01 40 41 20 20 🕑 Mon–Wed, Fri–Sat 9:30–7; Thu 9:30AM–10PM 🍴 Cafeteria, restaurant 🚇 Pont Neuf 🦽 Free

SQUARE DU VERT GALANT
Quintessential river-level view of bridges and the Louvre, shaded by willows and stunning at sunset.
🚩 G6 ✉ place du Pont-Neuf 75001 🕑 Oct–Mar: daily 9–5:30. Apr–Sep: daily 9AM–10PM 🚇 Pont Neuf

TOUR MONTPARNASSE
The 59th floor of this 686-foot modern tower in Montparnasse offers sweeping vistas of the city. Movies on Paris are screened on the 56th floor.
🚩 F8 ✉ 33 Avenue du Maine 75015 ☎ 01 45 38 52 56 🕑 Oct–Mar: daily 9:30AM–10:30PM. Apr–Sep: daily 9:30AM–11:30PM 🍴 Bar, restaurant 🚇 Montparnasse, Bienvenue 🦽 Moderate

Pollution over Paris
The promised views over Paris do not always materialize as the capital is often hidden in haze trapped by the saucer-like shape of the Île de France. Measures taken since the mid-1970s have helped: in one decade industrial pollution was reduced by 50 percent and the replacement of coal by nuclear energy and gas further cleared the air. However, carbon-monoxide levels (from vehicle exhausts) often exceed European Union norms.

The view from Tour Montparnasse

CHILDREN'S ACTIVITIES

Le guignol

A juvenile crowd-puller dating back to the early 19th century is the *guignol*, an open-air puppet show held in several Parisian parks. You'll find them in summer on Wednesdays, weekends, and during school vacations at parks such as the Luxembourg, Montsouris, Buttes Chaumont, Champ de Mars, and the Jardin d'Acclimatation.

CIRQUE ALEXIS GRÜSS

Perennial favorite, with a new high-tech circus show.
A4 ✉ Allée de la Reine Marguerite, Bois de Boulogne 75016 ☎ 01 44 17 96 22 🕐 Shows on Wed, Sat, Sun and public holidays 🚇 Porte d'Orléans 💶 Very expensive

DISNEYLAND PARIS

Disney's mega resort is firmly established and adding new rides and attractions all the time.
✉ 77777 Marne-la-Vallée ☎ Recorded information: 01 60 30 60 30 🕐 Mon–Fri 10–6; Sat, Sun 9–8 (late nights in summer; inquire) 🍴 Cafés, restaurants 🚉 RER Line A Marne-la-Vallée-Chessy 💶 Very expensive

LA GÉODE

This cinema's hemispherical screen plunges viewers into the heart of the action with frequent showings of nature and science movies. Nearby are Le Cinaxe, a mobile film theater, and the Cité des Sciences et de l'Industrie (▶ 50), with other children's activities.
L2 ✉ 26 avenue Corentin Cariou 75019 ☎ 01 40 05 12 12 🕐 Sessions Tue–Sun 🍴 Cafés in park 🚇 Porte de la Villette 💶 Moderate

JARDIN D'ACCLIMATATION

A specially designed section of the Bois de Boulogne with puppet theater, playground, fairground, educational museum, "enchanted river," circus, zoo, and minitrain (leaves from Porte Maillot on Wed, Sat, Sun, and public holidays).
B4 ✉ Bois de Boulogne 75016 ☎ 01 40 67 90 82 🕐 Daily 10–6 🍴 Café 🚇 Les Sablons 💶 Inexpensive

PARC ASTÉRIX

Some 22 miles north of Paris, this very Gallic theme park is dedicated to the comic-strip hero Astérix. Animation, rides, games, and food.
✉ 60128 Plailly ☎ Bookings 34 34 03 44 62 🕐 Apr to mid-Oct: daily 10–6. July–Aug: 9:30–7 🍴 Cafés, restaurants 🚉 RER Line B, Roissy-Charles de Gaulle 💶 Very expensive

La Géode

FREE ATTRACTIONS

ARÈNES DE LUTÈCE
A partly ruined Gallo-Roman amphitheater now
favored by *boules*-playing retirees. Destroyed in
AD 280, it was restored in the early 1900s.
🏠 H7 ✉ Rue des Arènes 75005 🕐 Oct–Mar: daily 8–5:30.
Apr–Sep: daily 8AM–10PM 🚇 Jussieu

DROUOT RICHELIEU
Let yourself be tempted at Paris's main auction
rooms. A Persian carpet, a Louis XV commode, or a
bunch of cutlery may come under the hammer.
Auctions start at 2PM.
🏠 G4 ✉ 9 rue Drouot 75009 ☎ 01 48 00 20 20 🕐 Daily 11–6.
Closed Aug 🚇 Richelieu-Drouot

JARDIN DU PALAIS-ROYAL
Elegant 18th-century arcades surround this peaceful
formal garden and palace (now the Conseil d'État
and the Ministère de la Culture), redolent of
Revolutionary history. Daniel Buren's conceptual
striped columns occupy the Cour d'Honneur.
🏠 G5 ✉ Place du Palais-Royal 75001 🕐 Oct–Mar: daily
7:30AM–8:30PM. Apr–Sep: daily 7AM–11PM 🍴 Restaurants, tea room
🚇 Palais-Royal/Musée du Louvre

MÉMORIAL DE LA DÉPORTATION
In the Île de la Cité's eastern tip is a starkly designed
crypt lined with 200,000 quartz pebbles to commem-
orate French citizens deported by the Nazis.
🏠 H6 ✉ Square de l'Île de France 75004 🕐 Mon–Fri 8:30–5:30;
Sat, Sun 9–5:30 🚇 Cité

PALAIS DE JUSTICE
Follow in the footsteps of lawyers, judges, and crooks
down echoing corridors,
staircases, and
courtyards, and, if your
French is up to it, sit in
on a court case. This
former royal palace took
on its present function
during the Revolution.
🏠 H6 ✉ Boulevard du Palais
75001 ☎ 01 44 32 50 00
🕐 Mon–Fri 9–5 🚇 Cité

PAVILLON DE
L'ARSENAL
This strikingly designed
building houses well-conceived exhibitions on urban
Paris alongside a permanent display of the city's
architectural evolution.
🏠 J7 ✉ 21 boulevard Morland 75004 ☎ 01 42 76 33 97
🕐 Tue–Sat 10:30–6:30; Sun 11–7 🚇 Sully Morland

Bargain Paris
Nothing comes cheap in this city
of light. Still, although
gastronomy, official culture, and
history cost money, browsing at
the *bouquinistes* along the Seine,
picnicking on the river banks,
reading in the parks, exploring
back streets, and spinning hours
away for the cost of a coffee on a
terrasse are some of Paris's
bargains.

The Palais Royal

INTRIGUING STREETS

Cour du Commerce-Saint-André

A narrow cobbled passage tucked away on the Left Bank, the Cour du Commerce-Saint-André connects rue Saint-André-des-Arts with boulevard Saint-Germain and dates from 1776, though it incorporates a medieval tower. It became a hive of Revolutionary activity, with Marat printing pamphlets at No. 8, Danton installed at No. 20, and the anatomy professor Dr. Guillotin (inventor of that "philanthropic beheading machine") at No. 9.

Storefront on the rue des Rosiers

BOULEVARD DE ROCHECHOUART
Teeming with struggling immigrants. Impromptu markets, Tati (the palace of cheap clothes), or seedy sex shops, and a pervasive aroma of *merguez* and fries.
✚ H3 🚇 Barbès-Rochechouart

RUE DU CHERCHE-MIDI
César's sculpture on the rue de Sèvres crossroads marks out this typical Left Bank street, home to the famous Poîlane bakery (No. 8) and the Musée Hébert (No. 85). Main interest ends at the Boulevard Raspail.
✚ G7 🚇 Saint-Sulpice

RUE DU FAUBOURG SAINT-HONORÉ
Price tags and politics cohabit in this street of luxury. See Hermès' imaginative window dressing or salute the gendarmes in front of the Élysée Palace.
✚ F4–F5 🚇 Madeleine

RUE JACOB
Antique and interior-decoration shops monopolize this picturesque stretch. Make a 20-pace detour to the Musée Delacroix on the delightful place Furstemberg.
✚ G6 🚇 Saint-Germain-des-Prés

RUE MONSIEUR-LE-PRINCE
An uphill stretch lined with university bookstores, antique and ethnic shops, and a sprinkling of student restaurants. Sections of the medieval city wall are embedded in Nos. 41 and 47.
✚ G7 🚇 Odéon

RUE DES ROSIERS
Effervescent street at heart of Paris's Jewish quarter. Kosher butchers and restaurants, the old hammam, and Hebrew bookstores rub shoulders with designer boutiques. Quiets considerably on Saturdays.
✚ J6 🚇 Saint-Paul

RUE VIEILLE-DU-TEMPLE
The pulse of the hip Marais district, dense in bars, cafés, boutiques, and, farther north, the historic Hôtel Amelot-de-Bisseuil (No. 47), the Maison J Hérouët, the Hôtel de Rohan (No. 87), and the garden of the Musée Picasso (➤ 51).
✚ J6 🚇 Saint-Paul

PARIS
where to...

STAY

Luxury Hotels	62
Mid-Range Hotels	63
Budget Accommodations	64

EAT

Expensive Restaurants	66
Regional French Restaurants	67
Asian Restaurants	68
Arab Restaurants	69
Italian & Miscellaneous Restaurants	70
Brasseries & Bistros	72

SHOP

Department Stores	74
Food & Wine	75
Markets	76
Art & Antiques	77
Books & Records	78
Miscellaneous	79
Fashion	80

BE ENTERTAINED

Concerts, Jazz Clubs & Nightclubs	82
Bars & Special Film Theaters	84
Sports	86

LUXURY HOTELS

Expect to pay over 2,000FF for a single room in the luxury category.

Le Crillon

Whether you stay at the Ritz, the Crillon, the Meurice, the Bristol, or the Georges V, they all have their tales to tell, but that of the Crillon is perhaps the most momentous. This family mansion (still wholly French-owned by the Taittingers of champagne fame) managed to survive the Revolution despite having the guillotine on its doorstep. Mary Pickford and Douglas Fairbanks spent their honeymoon here.

LE CRILLON
Fabulous Parisian classic which reeks glamour, history, and major investments. Suites are almost the norm here.
➕ F5 ✉ 10 place de la Concorde 75008 ☎ 01 44 71 15 00; fax 01 44 71 15 02 🚇 Concorde

L'HÔTEL
A Parisian legend redolent of Oscar Wilde's last days. Kitsch piano-bar and restaurant, and some superb rooms.
➕ G6 ✉ 13 rue des Beaux Arts 75006 ☎ 01 43 25 27 22; fax 01 43 25 64 81 🚇 Mabillon

HÔTEL DU JEU DE PAUME
A small, delightful hotel carved out of a 17th-century royal tennis court. Tasteful rooms with beams and marble bathrooms; some duplex suites. No restaurant.
➕ J7 ✉ 54 rue Saint-Louis-en-l'Île 75004 ☎ 01 43 26 14 18; fax 01 40 46 02 76 🚇 Pont Marie

HÔTEL LUTETIA
A temple to art deco refurbished by Sonia Rykiel. Avoid the less expensive back rooms. Well located between Saint-Germain and Montparnasse.
➕ F7 ✉ 45 boulevard Raspail 75006 ☎ 01 49 54 46 46; fax 01 49 54 46 00 🚇 Sèvres-Babylone

HÔTEL MEURICE
Classically ornate luxury, once home to Salvador Dali and before that the Nazi HQ during the Occupation. Now well run by the CIGA group.
➕ G5 ✉ 228 rue de Rivoli 75001 ☎ 01 44 58 10 10; fax 01 44 58 10 15 🚇 Tuileries

HÔTEL MONTALEMBERT
A fashionable Left Bank hotel with a garden-patio, bar, and restaurant. Chic design details and well-appointed rooms. Popular with Americans.
➕ F6 ✉ 3 rue de Montalembert 75007 ☎ 01 45 49 68 68; fax 01 45 49 69 49 🚇 Rue du Bac

HÔTEL SAINTE BEUVE
Exclusive establishment between the heart of Montparnasse and the Luxembourg gardens. Period antiques mix happily with modern furnishings.
➕ G7 ✉ 9 rue Sainte-Beuve 75006 ☎ 01 45 48 20 07; fax 01 45 48 67 52 🚇 Notre-Dame des Champs

HÔTEL SAN RÉGIS
Convenient for the couturiers on avenue Montaigne. Elaborately decorated but modest in scale; popular with showbiz folk. Restaurant for hotel guests only.
➕ E5 ✉ 12 rue Jean-Goujon 75008 ☎ 01 44 95 16 16; fax 01 45 61 05 48 🚇 Champs-Élysées-Clemenceau

PAVILLON DE LA REINE
Set back from place des Vosges. Flowery courtyard and period decoration. No restaurant.
➕ J6 ✉ 28 place des Vosges, 75003 ☎ 01 42 77 96 40; fax 01 42 77 63 06 🚇 Chemin Vert Bréguet Sabin

MID-RANGE HOTELS

HÔTEL DE L'ABBAYE SAINT GERMAIN

This quaint, historic establishment was once a convent. Cobbled courtyard, elegant salons, terraced duplex rooms, and friendly staff.

🕇 G7 ⊠ 10 rue Cassette 75006 ☎ 01 45 44 38 11; fax 01 45 48 07 86 🚇 Saint-Sulpice

HÔTEL D'ANGLETERRE

Former 18th-century British embassy. Garden patio, spacious rooms where Hemingway once lived. Bar and piano lounge. No restaurant.

🕇 G6 ⊠ 44 rue Jacob 75006 ☎ 01 42 60 34 72; fax 01 42 60 16 93 🚇 Saint-Germain-des-Prés

HÔTEL BERGÈRE

A modern, air-conditioned hotel run by Best Western close to the Grands Boulevards. Reliable though anonymous service.

🕇 H4 ⊠ 34 rue Bergère 75009 ☎ 01 47 70 34 34; fax 01 47 70 36 36 🚇 Rue Montmartre

HÔTEL DUC DE SAINT-SIMON

Rather pricey but the antique furnishings and picturesque setting just off boulevard Saint-Germain justify it. Comfortable rooms, intimate atmosphere. Needs advance reservation.

🕇 F6 ⊠ 14 rue Saint-Simon 75007 ☎ 01 44 39 20 20; fax 01 45 48 68 25 🚇 Rue du Bac

HÔTEL LENOX

Popular with the design and fashion world. Chase T. S. Eliot's ghost and enjoy the restored, stylish 1930s bar.

🕇 G6 ⊠ 9 rue de l'Université 75007 ☎ 01 42 96 10 95; fax 01 42 61 52 83 🚇 Saint-Germain-des-Prés

HÔTEL DES MARRONIERS

Named after the chestnut trees that dominate the garden. Oak-beamed rooms; vaulted cellars converted to lounges. Ask for a room overlooking the garden.

🕇 G6 ⊠ 21 rue Jacob 75006 ☎ 01 43 25 30 60; fax 01 40 46 83 56 🚇 Saint-Germain-des-Prés

HÔTEL MOLIÈRE

On a quiet street near the Louvre and Opéra. Well-appointed, reasonably priced rooms, and helpful staff. No restaurant.

🕇 G5 ⊠ 21 rue Molière 75001 ☎ 01 42 96 22 01; fax 01 42 60 48 68 🚇 Pyramides, Palais-Royal

HÔTEL LA PERLE

Renovated 18th-century building on a quiet street near Saint-Germain. Charming breakfast patio, bar, and well-appointed rooms.

🕇 G6 ⊠ 14 rue des Canettes 75006 ☎ 01 43 29 10 10; fax 01 46 34 51 04 🚇 Mabillon

RÉSIDENCE LORD BYRON

Comfortable, classy 31-room hotel just off the Champs Élysées. Small garden and well-appointed, reasonably priced rooms.

🕇 E4 ⊠ 5 rue Châteaubriand 75008 ☎ 01 43 59 89 98; fax 01 42 89 46 04 🚇 George V

A moderately priced hotel will charge 600–1,200FF for a single room.

Three-star rating

All these three-star establishments are obvious favorites with business travelers, so it is virtually impossible to find rooms during trade-fair seasons such as May to early June and mid-September to October. In summer many offer discounts as their clientele shrinks. All rooms are equipped with color TV, direct-dial phone, private bath or shower rooms, minibar, and most with hair dryer. Air-conditioning is not standard, but elevators are common.

BUDGET ACCOMMODATIONS

You should be able to find a single room in a budget hotel for under 600FF.

Budget hotels

Gone are the heady days when Paris was peppered with atmospheric one-star hotels with their inimitable signs *"eau à tous les étages"* ("water on every floor"). Now there are bath or shower rooms with every bedroom, and correspondingly higher prices and smaller rooms. So don't expect much space in budget hotel rooms, but do expect breakfast and receptionists who speak a second language in every hotel with two or more stars.

GRAND HÔTEL MALHER
Family hotel with 31 well-equipped rooms; excellent location.
✚ J6 ✉ 5 rue Malher 75004 ☎ 01 42 72 60 92; fax 01 42 72 25 37 🚇 Saint-Paul

GRAND HÔTEL DE SUEZ
Fifty-room hotel in central location on busy boulevard. Good-value but lacks atmosphere.
✚ H6 ✉ 31 boulevard Saint-Michel 75005 ☎ 01 46 34 08 02; fax 01 40 51 79 44 🚇 Cluny-La Sorbonne

HÔTEL ANDRÉ GILL
Charming courtyard setting on quiet side street close to Pigalle. Renovated rooms, reasonably priced.
✚ G3 ✉ 4 rue André-Gill 75018 ☎ 01 42 62 48 48; fax 01 42 62 77 92 🚇 Pigalle

HÔTEL DU COLLÈGE DE FRANCE
Tranquil 29-room establishment near the Sorbonne. Some 6th-floor rooms offer a glimpse of Notre Dame.
✚ H7 ✉ 7 rue Thénard 75005 ☎ 01 43 26 78 36; fax 01 46 34 58 29 🚇 Maubert-Mutualité

HÔTEL ESMERALDA
Very popular dollhouse hotel near Notre Dame. Reasonably priced.
✚ H6 ✉ 4 rue Saint-Julien-le-Pauvre 75005 ☎ 01 43 54 19 20; fax 01 40 51 00 68 🚇 Saint-Michel

HÔTEL ISTRIA
Legendary Montparnasse hotel once frequented by Rilke, Duchamp, and Man Ray. Twenty-six atmospheric rooms and friendly staff.
✚ G8 ✉ 29 rue Campagne Première 75014 ☎ 01 43 20 91 82; fax 01 43 22 48 45 🚇 Raspail

HÔTEL JARDIN DES PLANTES
Pretty hotel overlooking the botanical gardens. Good facilities.
✚ H7 ✉ 5 rue Linné 75005 ☎ 01 47 07 06 20; fax 01 47 07 62 74 🚇 Jussieu

HÔTEL DU GRAND PRIEURÉ
Unpretentious, clean, and quite comfortable accommodation close to place de la République. All bedrooms have minibar, bath plus shower.
✚ K5 ✉ 20 rue de Grand Prieuré 75011 ☎ 01 47 00 74 14; fax 01 49 23 06 64 🚇 Oberkampf

HÔTEL LINDBERGH
Modernized hotel on a tranquil side street near busy crossroads and the shops of Saint-Germain. Well-equipped rooms and polyglot staff.
✚ F7 ✉ 5 rue Chomel 75007 ☎ 01 45 48 35 53; fax 01 45 49 31 48 🚇 Sèvres-Babylone

HÔTEL AGORA
Welcoming staff and charming top-floor rooms with sloping ceilings. Most rooms with shower and lavatory only.
✚ H5 ✉ 7 rue de la Cossonnerie 75001 ☎ 01 42 33 46 02; fax: 01 42 33 80 99 🚇 Les Halles

HÔTEL FLORA
Close to Gare du Nord and Gare de l'Est. The hotel offers functional

rooms, half with bath, half
with shower.
H4 ✉ 1-3 cour de la Ferme
Saint-Lazare 75010 ☎ 01 48
24 84 84; fax 01 48 00 91 03
Ⓜ Gare de l'Est

HÔTEL DE LA PLACE DES VOSGES
Charming 17th-century
town house in a quiet
street close to Place des
Vosges. Basic comforts,
excellent location.
J6 ✉ 12 rue de Birague
75004 ☎ 01 42 72 60 46;
fax 01 42 72 02 64 Ⓜ Bastille

HÔTEL PRIMA-LEPIC
Close to the Moulin
Rouge; well-decorated but
smallish rooms and a
courtyard-style reception
area.
G3 ✉ 29 rue Lepic 75018
☎ 01 46 06 44 64; fax 01 46 06
66 11 Ⓜ Abbesses, Blanche

HÔTEL RÉCAMIER
Tranquil, friendly
little hotel close to Saint-
Germain and the
Luxembourg gardens.
G7 ✉ 3 bis place Saint-
Sulpice 75006 ☎ 01 43 26
04 89 Ⓜ Saint-Sulpice

HÔTEL DE ROUEN
Very cheap 22-room hotel
with surprisingly well-
equipped rooms. Central
location near the Louvre
and Palais Royal.
G5 ✉ 42 rue Croix-des-
Petits-Champs 75001 ☎ fax 01
42 61 38 21 Ⓜ Louvre-Rivoli

HÔTEL DU 7E ART
Cinephiles' hotel
decorated with movie
photos and memorabilia.
Great location in the
Marais and reasonably
priced rooms.
J6 ✉ 20 rue Saint-Paul

75004 ☎ 01 42 77 04 03; fax
01 42 77 69 10 Ⓜ Saint-Paul

HÔTEL SOLFÉRINO
A rare budget hotel in the
chic 7th. Antique
furniture. Opposite Musée
d'Orsay on quiet street.
Excellent value.
F6 ✉ 91 rue de Lille
75007 ☎ 01 47 05 85 54; fax
01 45 55 51 16 Ⓜ Solférino

HÔTEL DE LA SORBONNE
On a quiet side street near
the Sorbonne. Small but
comfortable rooms. Well
established and
unpretentious.
H7 ✉ 6 rue Victor-Cousin
75005 ☎ 01 43 54 58 08;
fax 01 40 51 05 18
Ⓜ Cluny-La Sorbonne

HÔTEL DU VIEUX SAULE
On a quiet street north of
Marais. Modernized, with
reasonable facilities.
J5 ✉ 6 rue de Picardie
75003 ☎ 01 42 72 01 14;
fax 01 40 27 88 21
Ⓜ Filles du Calvaire

SUPER HÔTEL
Near Père Lachaise
cemetery. Good , easy
transportation,
comfortable rooms.
M5 ✉ 208 rue des
Pyrénées 75020 ☎ 01 46 36
97 48; fax 01 46 36 26 10
Ⓜ Gambetta

TIMHÔTEL LE LOUVRE
One of small chain with
reliable amenities and
reasonably priced
rooms. Well situated for
Louvre and Les Halles.
G5 ✉ 4 rue
Croix-des-Petits-Champs 75001
☎ 01 42 60 34 86; fax 01 42
60 10 39 Ⓜ Louvre-Rivoli

Bed and breakfast
For those staying longer than
one night, renting an apartment
makes good financial sense. The
Apartment Service offers a wide
selection of deluxe and standard
apartments throughout central
Paris.
☎ +44 181 944 1444
fax + 44 181 944 6744
email: res@apartment.co.uk
Internet: www.apartment.co.uk
For bed and breakfast, staying
with host families, try France
Lodge, 41 rue la Fayette 75009,
or International Café Couette, 8
rue d'Isly 75008

EXPENSIVE RESTAURANTS

The restaurants on the following pages are in three price categories:

SSS   over 500FF per person

SS   up to 500FF per person

S   up to 150FF per person

Rose-tinted dining

Le Pré Catelan (SSS) has an elegant setting near the rose gardens of the Parc Bagatelle, and both indoor and outdoor seating. Precise, sophisticated modern cooking and exquisite desserts (✉ Bois de Boulogne, Route de Suresnes 75016 ☎ 01 44 14 41 14).

ALAIN DUCASSE ($$$)
Alain Ducasse offers updated versions of the great culinary classics at his gastronomic mecca.
✚ C5 ✉ 59 avenue Raymond-Poincaré 75116 ☎ 01 47 27 12 27 🕐 Closed Sat–Sun, Jul 🚇 Trocadéro

ARPÈGE ($$$)
Decor is slightly minimalist and Alain Passard's cooking glows with distinctive originality.
✚ F6 ✉ 84 rue de Varenne 75007 ☎ 01 45 51 47 33 🕐 Closed Sat, Sun lunch, Aug 🚇 Varenne

CARRÉ DES FEUILLANTS ($$$)
Elegant setting for Alain Dutournier's brilliant evocation of the cooking of his beloved native Gascony. He uses the best-possible ingredients to marvellous effect.
✚ F5–G5 ✉ 14 rue de Castiglione 75001 ☎ 01 42 86 82 82 🕐 Closed Sat lunch, Sun, Aug 🚇 Tuileries

GUY SAVOY ($$$)
One of the city's gastronomic temples where Guy Savoy cooks in a refreshingly simple style.
✚ D4 ✉ 18 rue Troyon 75017 ☎ 01 43 80 40 61 🕐 Closed Sat–Sun 🚇 Charles de Gaulle-Étoile

LUCAS-CARTON ($$$)
Stunning belle-époque restaurant that's home to Alain Sendeens' exquisite, but expensive, cooking. Lunch is good value.
✚ F5 ✉ 9 place de la Madeleine 75008 ☎ 01 42 65 22 90 🕐 Closed Sat–Sun, Aug, Dec 24, Jan 3 🚇 Madeleine

PIERRE GAGNAIRE ($$$)
Here you'll find extraordinary cooking from one of France's, and even the world's, greatest culinary geniuses. Reserve very well in advance.
✚ D4 ✉ 6 rue de Balzac 75008 ☎ 01 44 35 18 25 🕐 Closed Sat, Sun lunch, Aug 🚇 George V

MICHEL ROSTANG ($$$)
Rostang still holds his own in the Parisian gastronomy stakes with cooking that's bursting with life and invention. Marvelous desserts.
✚ D3 ✉ 20 rue Rennequin 75017 ☎ 01 47 63 40 77 🕐 Closed Sun, Aug 🚇 Ternes

TAILLEVENT ($$$)
Refined restaurant with an elegant, club-like ambience. The cooking has solid, classical foundations, with subtle contemporary leanings. Superlative wine list.
✚ E4 ✉ 15 rue Lamennais 75008 ☎ 01 44 95 15 01 🕐 Closed Sat, Sun, Aug 🚇 George V

LA TOUR D'ARGENT ($$$)
Historic restaurant best known for duck, including the specialty duck à la presse with cherries. Fabulous view, and great wine cellar.
✚ H7 ✉ 15–17 quai de la Tournelle 75005 ☎ 01 43 54 23 31 🕐 Closed Mon 🚇 Saint-Paul

REGIONAL FRENCH RESTAURANTS

L'AMBASSADE D'AUVERGNE ($$)
Rustic decor and authentic, robust farmhouse cooking from the Auvergne region.
⊞ H5 ✉ 22 rue du Grenier Saint Lazare 75003 ☎ 01 42 72 31 22 🕐 Closed Aug 🚇 Rambuteau

AUBERGE BRESSANE ($/$$)
Delectable dishes from eastern France, and an impressive wine list of Bordeaux and Burgundies. Mock medieval setting. Excellent-value lunches.
⊞ E6 ✉ 16 avenue de la Motte Picquet 75007 ☎ 01 47 05 98 37 🕐 Closed Sat lunch 🚇 La Tour-Maubourg

AU TROU GASCON ($$$)
1900 bistro-style setting for wonderful southwest cooking. The cassoulet is among the finest in Paris, with homemade sausages and beans from Tarbes.
⊞ L8 ✉ 40 rue Taine 75012 ☎ 01 43 44 34 26 🕐 Closed Sat lunch, Sun, Aug 🚇 Daumesnil

LA BARACANE ($$)
Tiny, tastefully decorated restaurant whose menu homes in on Gascony and duck.
⊞ J6 ✉ 38 rue des Tournelles 75004 ☎ 01 42 71 43 33 🕐 Closed Sat lunch, Sun 🚇 Bastille

BRASSERIE FLO ($$)
Characterful Alsatian brasserie that dishes up mountains of delicious *choucroute spéciale*. Noisy, popular, and chaotic.
⊞ H4 ✉ 7 cour des Petites Ecuries 75010 ☎ 01 47 70 13 59 🕐 Daily until 1AM 🚇 Château d'Eau

LE CAVEAU DU PALAIS ($$)
A long-established restaurant offering traditional, competent cooking. Dishes vary according to season.
⊞ G6 ✉ 17/19 place Dauphine 75001 ☎ 01 43 26 04 28 🕐 Closed Sat, Sun 🚇 Pont Neuf

CHEZ BENOIT ($$$)
Long-standing favorite, serving classic regional dishes. Reserve ahead.
⊞ H5 ✉ 20 rue Saint-Martin 75004 ☎ 01 42 72 25 76 🕐 Daily 🚇 Châtelet

LE CROQUANT ($$)
Intriguing, and well-thought out modern interpretations of southwest classics.
⊞ C8 ✉ 28 rue Jean-Maridor 75015 ☎ 01 45 58 50 83 🕐 Closed Sat lunch, mid-Jul to mid-Aug, Sun eve, Mon 🚇 Lourmel

CAMPAGNE ET PROVENCE ($$)
Sunny Provençal cooking in an intimate, yet cheerful setting by the Seine. Good selection of wines from Provence.
⊞ H7 ✉ 25 quai de la Tournelle 75005 ☎ 01 43 54 05 17 🕐 Closed Sat lunch, Sun, Aug 🚇 Maubert-Mutualité

LOUS LANDES ($$)
A genial atmosphere, and a menu of traditional dishes from the southwest.
⊞ F9 ✉ 157 avenue du Maine 75014 ☎ 01 45 43 08 04 🕐 Closed Sat lunch, Sun, Aug 🚇 Mouton-Duvernet

French mean cuisine

"The only cooks in the civilized world are French. Other races have different interpretations of food. Only the French mean *cuisine* because their qualities— rapidity, decision-making, tact— are used. Who has ever seen a foreigner succeed in making a white sauce?"

—Nestor Roqueplan (1804–70), Editor of *Le Figaro*.

ASIAN RESTAURANTS

The 13th *arrondissement*

The Paris Chinese community is spread through Belleville, where it coexists with Arabs and Africans; through the 3rd *arrondissement*, where invisible sweatshops churn out cheap leather goods; and above all through the 13th *arrondissement* (🚇 Tolbiac, Porte d'Ivry). At the latter, Chinese New Year is celebrated with dragon parades in late January or early February. The area offers a fantastic array of Indochinese and Chinese restaurants and soup kitchens—all at budget prices.

RESTAURANT A ($$)
Classical Chinese dishes, many from the Imperial Court, artistically prepared for an appreciative, mainly local, crowd.
🚇 H7 ✉ 5 rue de Poissy 75005 ☎ 01 46 33 85 54
⏰ Closed Mon lunch
🚇 Maubert-Mutualité

BENKAY ($$$)
A modern Japanese restaurant with panoramic views from the 4th floor of the Hotel Nikko de Paris. Good *teppanyaki*. The set lunch menus are reasonably priced.
🚇 C7 ✉ quai de Grenelle 75015 ☎ 01 40 58 21 26
⏰ Daily 🚇 Bir Hakeim

CHEZ ROSINE ($$)
Succulent, imaginative Cambodian dishes orchestrated by charismatic Rosine Ek.
🚇 G5 ✉ 12 rue du Mont Thabor 75001 ☎ 01 49 27 09 23 ⏰ Closed Sun, Mon lunch
🚇 Tuileries

CHIENG-MAI ($$)
Elegant Thai restaurant, and one of the best in town, with charming service and subtle food. Popular, so reserve.
🚇 H7 ✉ 12 rue Frédéric-Sauton 75005 ☎ 01 43 25 45 45 ⏰ Closed Sun, part of Aug
🚇 Maubert-Mutualité

FOC-LY ($$)
Smart, comfortable restaurant specializing in Chinese and Thai cooking. Spicing is generally mild and service friendly and efficient.
🚇 E7 ✉ 71 avenue de Sufren 75007 ☎ 01 47 83 27 12
⏰ Closed Mon in Aug
🚇 La Motte-Picquet-Grenelle

KAPPA ($$)
Well-established *sushi* restaurant with a warm, animated atmosphere.
🚇 G6 ✉ 6 rue des Ciseaux 75006 ☎ 01 43 26 33 31
⏰ Closed Sun
🚇 Saint-Germain-des-Prés

KIM ANH ($$)
Tiny restaurant with exotic decor, serving some of Paris's best Vietnamese food. The owner's wife specializes in the cooking of her native Saigon
🚇 C7 ✉ 15 rue de l'Église 75015 ☎ 01 45 79 40 96
⏰ Daily 🚇 Charles-Michels

NEW NIOULLAVILLE ($)
Vast Hong Kong-style restaurant with a long menu of Chinese, Laotian, Thai, and Vietnamese specialties.
🚇 K4 ✉ 32–34 rue de l'Orillon 75011 ☎ 01 43 38 95 23 ⏰ Closed Sun evening
🚇 Belleville

TAN DINH ($$)
Vietnamese cuisine, in an elegantly designed restaurant situated just behind the Musée d'Orsay. Impressive wine list and polished service.
🚇 F6 ✉ 60 rue de Verneuil 75007 ☎ 01 45 44 04 84
⏰ Closed Sun, Aug
🚇 Rue du Bac

YUGARAJ ($$)
One of Paris's best Indian restaurants. Discreet and elegant, with friendly Sri Lankan waiters. Spicing is mild.
🚇 G6 ✉ 14 rue Dauphine 75006 ☎ 01 43 26 44 91
⏰ Closed Mon lunch
🚇 Pont Neuf

ARAB RESTAURANTS

AL DAR ($$)
Luxurious Lebanese restaurant, with a terrific selection of *mezze*, and excellent couscous. Takeout section.
➕ H7 ✉ 8–10 rue Frédéric-Sauton 75005 ☎ 01 43 25 17 15 🕐 Daily
Ⓜ Maubert-Mutualité

L'ATLAS ($$)
Fabulous kitsch juxtaposition of Louis XIII chairs and Moroccan mosaics. Modern interpretations of sophisticated North African cooking served with genuine smiles.
➕ H7 ✉ 12 boulevard Saint-Germain 75005
☎ 01 46 33 86 98 🕐 Daily
Ⓜ Maubert-Mutualité

CHEZ OMAR ($)
Generous couscous and grilled meats in a friendly, spacious, and buzzing setting. Popular; reserve for dinner or arrive early.
➕ J5 ✉ 47 rue de Bretagne 75003 ☎ 01 42 72 36 26
🕐 Closed Sun lunch Ⓜ Arts et Métiers

FAKHR EL DINE ($$)
Spacious Lebanese restaurant with smart decor. On offer are traditional specialties from *tabbouleh* to lamb *brochettes*.
➕ D5 ✉ 1–3 rue Quentin-Bauchart 75008 ☎ 01 47 23 44 42 🕐 Daily Ⓜ George V

LE MANSOURIA ($$)
Authentic Moroccan restaurant offering some of the city's best couscous and *pastilla*. Often crowded.
➕ L7 ✉ 11 rue Faidherbe 75011 ☎ 01 43 71 00 16
🕐 Closed Mon lunch
Ⓜ Faidherbe Chaligny

NOURA ($$)
Stylish, busy Lebanese snack bar with takeout service, brother of the plush Pavillon Noura (☎ 01 47 20 33 33) down the road.
➕ D4 ✉ 27 avenue Marceau 75116 ☎ 01 47 23 02 20
🕐 Daily Ⓜ Charles de Gaulle-Étoile

TIMGAD ($$$)
One of the best-known Arab restaurants in France. Spectacular Moorish decor. Delicate *pastilla*, perfect couscous, attentive service. Reserve ahead.
➕ D4 ✉ 21 rue Brunel 75017 ☎ 01 45 74 23 70 🕐 Daily
Ⓜ Argentine

WALLY EL SAHARIEN ($$)
Wally Chouaki offers a wonderful choice of *harira*, *pastilla*, stuffed sardines, and, of course, couscous (Saharan). Delicate sweet pastries to finish.
➕ H3 ✉ 36 rue Rodier 75009 ☎ 01 42 85 51 90
🕐 Closed Mon lunch, Sun
Ⓜ Anvers

404 ($$)
In the same ownership as Momo off London's Regent Street, this very fashionable Moroccan restaurant with its chic Berber decor offers excellent North African cuisine.
➕ J5 ✉ 64 rue des Gravilliers 75003 ☎ 01 42 74 57 81
🕐 Closed Sun eve, Aug
Ⓜ Arts et Métiers

Couscous and *tajine*

Couscous is a mound of steamed semolina that is accompanied by a tureen of freshly cooked vegetables (onion, tomato, carrot, potato, zucchini) and the meat (or not) of your choice, from grilled lamb kebabs (*brochettes*) to chicken or *merguez* (spicy sausages). *Tajine* is a delicious stew, traditionally cooked in a covered terracotta dish, that may combine lamb and prunes, or chicken, pickled lemon, and olives.

ITALIAN AND MISCELLANEOUS RESTAURANTS

Pharamond

Alexandre Pharamond served his first plate of *tripes à la mode de Caen* in 1870, two doors from the site of the present restaurant, a sanctuary for lovers of tripe, pigs' trotters, and *andouillette*. It was entirely redecorated for the 1900 Exposition Universelle, and most of this structure and decoration has been preserved. The pretty floral and vegetal friezes that cover the walls of the rooms once adorned the entire four-story façade. Prices are high and reservation is essential (✚ H5 ✉ 24 rue de la Grande Truanderie 75001 ☎ 01 42 33 06 72 🕐 Closed Mon lunch, Sun, Jul 🚇 Les Halles).

ITALIAN

CASA BINI ($$)

Chic but relaxed Tuscan-style trattoria specializes in north Italian dishes.
✚ G6 ✉ 36 rue Grégoire-de-Tours 75006 ☎ 01 46 34 05 60 🕐 Closed Sat, Sun lunch 🚇 Odéon

CHEZ VINCENT ($$)

Authentic trattoria with colorful decor and a menu that offers *antipasti* and mini pizzas to die for.
✚ L3 ✉ 5 rue du Tunnel 75019 ☎ 01 42 02 22 45 🕐 Closed Sat lunch, Sun 🚇 Botzaris

LA ROMANTICA ($$)

Brilliant cooking at this off-the-beaten-track restaurant. Superb wine list and stunning terrace for alfresco dining.
✚ E1 ✉ 73 boulevard Jean-Jaurès 92110 Clichy ☎ 01 47 37 29 71 🕐 Closed Sat lunch, Sun 🚇 Mairie-de-Clichy

PAOLO PETRINI ($$)

A seasonal menu of classic cooking prepared to order from the finest ingredients makes for one of the city's best Italian restaurants.
✚ C4 ✉ 6 rue du Débarcadère ☎ 01 45 74 25 95 🕐 Daily 🚇 Porte Maillot

SIPARIO ($$)

Theatrically styled restaurant near the Opéra de Paris-Bastille. Inventive pasta, seafood, and meat dishes.
✚ K7 ✉ 69 rue de Charenton 75011 ☎ 01 43 45 70 26 🕐 Closed Sun 🚇 Bastille

SORMANI ($$$)

Just north of the Arc de Triomphe, this elegant restaurant, renowned for inspirational modern cooking, is a favorite with wealthy Parisians.
✚ D4 ✉ 4 rue du Général-de-Lanrezac 75017 ☎ 01 43 80 13 91 🕐 Closed Sat, Sun, Aug 🚇 Charles de Gaulle-Étoile

STRESA ($$)

Fashionable isn't the word. Couturiers drop in here for a quick pasta or risotto. Run with gusto by Neapolitan twins. Reserve ahead.
✚ E5 ✉ 7 rue de Chambiges 75008 ☎ 01 47 23 51 62 🕐 Closed dinner Sat, Sun 🚇 Alma, Marceau

MISCELLANEOUS

LES BOOKINISTES ($$)

Very trendy and successful restaurant owned by Guy Savoy. Innovation goes hand-in-hand with attention to detail.
✚ G6 ✉ 53 quai des Grands Augustins 75006 ☎ 01 42 25 45 94 🕐 Closed lunch Sat & Sun 🚇 Saint-Michel

MA BOURGOGNE ($$)

Hearty, unpretentious food perfect for a summer lunch or dinner. Or just stop for a drink.
✚ J6 ✉ 19 place des Vosges 75004 ☎ 01 42 78 44 64 🕐 Daily. Closed Feb 🚇 Chemin Vert

CAFÉ DE L'INDUSTRIE ($)

Spacious, relaxed café-restaurant-tea room; 1970s atmosphere, rock music. Open until 1:30AM with simple, reasonable food.
✚ K6 ✉ 16 rue Saint-Sabin 75011 ☎ 01 47 00 13 53 🕐 Closed Sat 🚇 Bastille

ECAILLE ET PLUME ($$)

Fish and game are the specialties of this romantic candlelit restaurant.

⊞ E6 ✉ 25 rue Duvivier 75007 ☎ 01 45 55 06 72 🕐 Closed Sat lunch, Sun, Aug 🚇 École Militaire

FAUCHON – LE 30 ($$)

On the second floor of one of the world's finest food shops, this elegant restaurant, with pretty terrace, is super for lunch.

⊞ F4 ✉ 30 place de la Madeleine 75008 ☎ 01 47 42 56 58 🕐 Closed Sun 🚇 Madeleine

LE FOUQUET'S ($$)

A Parisian institution on the Champs Élysées and a place to see and be seen. A snack menu operates all day in the bar or on the terrace.

⊞ E4 ✉ 9 avenue des Champs-Élysées 75008 ☎ 01 47 23 70 60 🕐 Daily 🚇 George V

LA GALERIE ($)

Pleasant relief from the Montmartre tourist haunts. Set lunch and dinner menus are very good value. Cheerful and friendly.

⊞ G3 ✉ 16 rue Tholozé 75018 ☎ 01 42 59 25 76 🕐 Closed Sun 🚇 Abbesses

GAYA RIVE GAUCHE ($$)

More fashionable sister to Gaya Rive Drome in rue Duphot. The best and freshest fish is prepared in an uncomplicated manner.

⊞ F6 ✉ 44 rue du Bac 75007 ☎ 01 45 44 73 73 🕐 Closed Sun, 2 weeks Aug 🚇 Rue du Bac

LA GUEUZE ($)

A few paces from the Jardin du Luxembourg, the specialty here is Belgian food and an amazing selection of beers.

⊞ H7 ✉ 19 rue Soufflot 75005 ☎ 01 43 54 63 00 🕐 Daily (Fri, Sat till 4.30AM) 🚇 Cluny la Sorbonne

JOE ALLEN ($)

Reliable hamburger-based fare served with humor and background music in a still fashionable late-night haunt in Les Halles.

⊞ H5 ✉ 30 rue Pierre-Lescot 75001 ☎ 01 42 36 70 13 🕐 Daily 🚇 Étienne-Marcel

MICHEL COURTALHAC ($$)

Close to the Assemblée Nationale, a simple, attractive restaurant offering delicious market-fresh foods.

⊞ F6 ✉ 47 rue de Bourgogne 75007 ☎ 01 45 55 15 35 🕐 Closed Sat lunch, Sun, Aug 🚇 Varenne

LA ROTISSERIE D'EN FACE ($$)

Across the road from Jacques Cagna's main restaurant, the setting here is lively, modern, and informal. Delicious free-range chicken.

⊞ G6 ✉ 2 rue Christine 75006 ☎ 01 43 26 40 98 🕐 Closed Sat lunch, Sun 🚇 Odéon, Saint-Michel

WILLI'S WINE BAR ($$)

Cheerful, British-owned restaurant/wine bar with an extensive wine list and fresh cuisine.

⊞ G5 ✉ 13 rue des Petits Champs 75001 ☎ 01 42 61 05 09 🕐 Closed Sun 🚇 Palais-

Culinary connections

It is said that Cathérine de Médicis, the Italian wife of Henri II, invented French cuisine in the 16th century—though Gallic opinions may differ. Italian cuisine in today's Paris is, not surprisingly, very much a pizza-pasta affair, and authentic dishes are rare.

BRASSERIES & BISTROS

La Coupole

Horror struck Parisian hearts in the mid-1980s when it was announced that La Coupole had been bought by property developers and several floors were to be added on top. This happened, but the famous old murals (by Juan Gris, Soutine, Chagall, Delaunay, and many more) have been reinstated, the red-velvet seats preserved, and the art-deco lights duly restored. The 1920s interior is now a historic monument.

L'ARBUCI ($$)
Jazz in the basement and splendid seafood upstairs, including oysters *à volonté*—you may eat as much as you want.
⊞ G6 ✉ 25 rue de Buci 75006 ☎ 01 44 32 16 00 🕐 Open till 2AM daily 🚇 Mabillon

BATIFOL ($)
One of a chain of good, inexpensive, traditional bistros that are open long hours.
⊞ J5 ✉ 15 place de la République 75003 ☎ 01 48 04 02 12 🕐 Daily till midnight 🚇 République

BISTRO D'À CÔTÉ ($$)
One of Michel Rostang's three successful more budget-conscious restaurants serving modern versions of traditional dishes.
⊞ H7 ✉ 16 boulevard Saint-Germain 75005 ☎ 01 43 54 59 10 🕐 Daily 🚇 Maubert-Mutualité

BISTROT DU SOMMELIER ($$)
Phenomenal wine list from the winner of the World's Best Sommelier award. The food is good but almost takes second place.
⊞ F4 ✉ 97 boulevard Haussmann 75008 ☎ 01 42 65 24 85 🕐 Closed Sat, Sun, Aug 🚇 Saint-Augustin, Miromesnil

CHEZ CATHERINE ($)
Charming long-established bistro that is conveniently close to the boulevard Haussmann department stores.
⊞ G4 ✉ 65 rue de Provence 75009 ☎ 01 45 26 72 88

🕐 Closed Sat, Sun, Mon eve, 1st week Jan 🚇 Chaussée d'Antin, La Fayette

LE BALZAR ($$)
Fashionable brasserie near the Sorbonne. Seafood, pigs' trotters, *cassoulet*. Camus and Sartre had their last argument here.
⊞ H7 ✉ 49 rue des Ecoles 75005 ☎ 01 43 54 13 67 🕐 Closed Aug 🚇 Cluny, La Sorbonne

BOFINGER ($$)
Claims to be Paris's oldest brasserie (1864). Soaring glass dome, lots of mirrors, and chandeliers. Seafood, *choucroute*, and steaks.
⊞ K6 ✉ 5 rue de la Bastille 75004 ☎ 01 42 72 87 82 🕐 Daily 🚇 Bastille

BRASSERIE LIPP ($$)
Probably Paris's most famous brasserie, founded in 1880. It was, and is, a haunt of the famous.
⊞ G6 ✉ 151 boulevard Saint-Germain 75006 ☎ 01 45 48 53 91 🕐 Closed Aug 🚇 Saint-Germain-des-Prés

BRASSERIE STELLA ($$)
Original 1950s decor in heart of the chic 16th *arrondissement*. Seafood, oysters, and wines from Sancerre and Beaujolais.
⊞ C5 ✉ 133 avenue Victor-Hugo 75016 ☎ 01 47 27 60 54 🕐 Daily 🚇 Victor Hugo

CHEZ PAUL ($$)
A mecca for Bastille art-dealers and artists, with delicious stuffed rabbit and *steak tartare*. Essential to reserve.
⊞ K6 ✉ 13 rue de Charonne 75011 ☎ 01 47 00 34 57 🕐 Daily 🚇 Ledru Rollin

LE COUDE FOU ($$)
Popular Marais bistro with hearty classics. Excellent wine list.
➕ J6 ✉ 12 rue du Bourg Tibourg 75004 ☎ 01 42 77 15 16 🍴 Closed Sun lunch 🚇 Hôtel de Ville

LA COUPOLE ($$)
A Montparnasse institution dating from the 1920s. Wide choice of brasserie food, reasonable late-night menu (after 11PM).
➕ F7 ✉ 102 boulevard du Montparnasse 75014 ☎ 01 43 20 14 20 🍴 Daily 🚇 Vavin

LE DEPART DE SAINT MICHEL ($)
All-hours brasserie at a very busy crossroads by the Seine. Great for people watching and *croques*.
➕ H6 ✉ 1 place Saint-Michel 75005 ☎ 01 43 54 24 53 🚇 Saint-Michel

L'ÉPI DUPIN ($$)
Chef/patron François Pasteau presents incredible and reasonably priced four-course menus in a 17th-century setting.
➕ F7 ✉ 11 rue Dupin 75006 ☎ 01 42 22 64 56 🍴 Closed Sat, Sun 🚇 Sèvres-Babylone

LE GRAND COLBERT ($$)
Restored 19th-century brasserie opening on to the Galerie Colbert. Good seafood and a cheerful atmosphere.
➕ G5 ✉ 2 rue Vivienne 75002 ☎ 01 42 86 87 88 🍴 Daily 🚇 Bourse

MARTY ($$)
First-floor 1930s-style brasserie offering

deliciously fresh shellfish and other seafood as well as a few good meat dishes.
➕ H8 ✉ 20 avenue des Gobelins 75005 ☎ 01 43 31 39 51 🍴 Daily 🚇 Les Gobelins

AU PETIT RICHE ($$)
Wonderful old 1880s bistro. Reliable traditional cuisine and good Loire wines.
➕ G4 ✉ 25 rue Le Peletier 75009 ☎ 01 47 70 68 68 🍴 Closed Sun 🚇 Richelieu-Drouot

LE PETIT SAINT-BENOÎT ($)
Popular old Saint-Germain classic; decor barely changed since the 1930s. Outside tables in summer.
➕ G6 ✉ 4 rue Saint-Benoît 75006 ☎ 01 42 60 27 92 🍴 Closed Sun 🚇 Saint-Germain-des-Prés

AU PIED DE COCHON ($$)
Open every day and every night, a convivial brasserie serving classic fare, including their renowned pigs' trotters.
➕ H5 ✉ 6 rue Coquillère 75001 ☎ 01 40 13 77 00 🍴 Open 24 hours 🚇 Les Halles

LA ROTISSERIE DU BEAUJOLAIS ($$)
Quayside bistro with a view of Notre Dame and in the same ownership as La Tour d'Argent across the road.
➕ H7 ✉ 19 quai de la Tournelle 75005 ☎ 01 43 54 17 47 🍴 Closed Mon 🚇 Maubert-Mutualité

Alsace and the southwest
Gastronomically speaking, Alsace and the southwest are probably the best-represented regions in Paris. Numerous brasseries churn out *choucroute* (sauerkraut), but it is the southwest that carries off the prizes with its variations on goose and duck. Recent research has found that inhabitants of this region have unexpectedly low rates of cardiac disease— despite their daily consumption of cholesterol-high *foie gras*.

DEPARTMENT STORES

Opening hours

Parisian opening hours follow a Monday–Saturday pattern. Smaller stores generally open by 10AM, sometimes closing for lunch, and shut at 7PM. Avoid shopping on Saturdays when every citizen seems to hit the streets, and take advantage of department store late-opening nights. Chain stores such as Prisunic and Monoprix are useful when you need inexpensive household goods and even fashion accessories.

BHV (BAZAR DE L'HÔTEL DE VILLE)
The do-it-yourself mecca. Browse among the basement nuts and bolts, classic clothes, and accessories on the first floor.
✚ H6 ✉ 52–64 rue de Rivoli 75004 ☎ 01 42 74 90 00 🕐 Mon, Tue, Thu–Sat 9:30–7; Wed 9:30AM–10PM 🚇 Hôtel de Ville

AU BON MARCHÉ RIVE GAUCHE
Very *BCBG* (*bon chic bon genre*). Gourmet foods, designer clothes, household linens, and haberdashery. Excellent basement bookstore.
✚ F7 ✉ 22 rue de Sèvres 75007 ☎ 01 44 39 80 00 🕐 Mon–Sat 9:30–7 🚇 Sèvres-Babylone

FORUM DES HALLES
Underground complex on four levels where some 50 small ready-to-wear designers have their boutiques.
✚ H5 ✉ 1–7 rue Pierre-Lescot 75001 ☎ 01 44 76 96 56 🚇 Châtelet, Les Halles

GALERIES LAFAYETTE
Under a giant glass dome, an enticing display of everything a home and its inhabitants need. Marginally better quality and pricier than Printemps. Top fashion designers are all represented and accessories are endless. Smaller branch near the Tour Montparnasse.
✚ G4 ✉ 40 boulevard Haussmann 75009 ☎ 01 42 82 34 56 🕐 Mon–Wed, Fri, Sat 9:30–6:45; Thu 9:30–9 🚇 Chaussée d'Antin

MARKS & SPENCER
Food, clothes, household goods, excellent wines. There is another branch of this very British store at 35 boulevard Haussmann 75009 (01 47 42 42 91).
✚ H6 ✉ 88 rue de Rivoli 75004 ☎ 01 44 61 08 00 🕐 Mon–Fri 10–8; Sat 10–7:30 🚇 Châtelet, Hôtel de Ville

PRINTEMPS
A classic for men's and women's fashions, accessories, household goods, furniture, designer gadgets, and more. Budget-conscious fashion-victims should look for the store's own collection: *Sélection Printemps*.
✚ G4 ✉ 64 boulevard Haussmann 75009 ☎ 01 42 82 50 00 🕐 Mon–Wed, Fri, Sat 9:35–7; Thu till 10 🚇 Havre-Caumartin

SAMARITAINE
Labyrinthine store largely occupying a superb 1904 construction. Fashion is so so, but other departments are great. Good basement hardware section, and a useful separate store for sports equipment and clothes.
✚ H6 ✉ 19 rue de la Monnaie 75001 ☎ 01 40 41 20 20 🕐 Mon–Wed, Fri, Sat 9:30–7; Thu till 10 🚇 Pont Neuf

TATI
Originally aimed at the emptiest purses in Paris, Tati now attracts the rich and famous but is still low cost. Women's, men's, and children's clothes, as well as household goods.
✚ H3 ✉ 2–30 boulevard Rochechouart 75018 ☎ 01 42 55 13 09 🚇 Barbès-Rochechouart

FOOD & WINE

ANDROUET

Encyclopedic range of pungent French cheeses in perfectly ripened states. Cheese restaurant attached; delivery service in Paris.

 F3 ✉ 41 6 rue Arsène-Houssar 75008 ☎ 01 42 89 95 00 Ⓜ Charles de Gaulle-Étoile

CHARCUTERIE LYONNAISE

The specialties of Lyon, including sublime *jambon persille* and sausages.

F4 ✉ 58 rue des Martyrs 75009 ☎ 01 48 78 96 45 Ⓜ Notre Dame de Lorette

FAUCHON

The gourmet's paradise—at a price. Established luxury delicatessen offering only the best in spices, exotic fruit, tea, coffee, charcuterie, pâtisseries… and more.

F5 ✉ 26 place de la Madeleine 75008 ☎ 01 47 42 60 11 Ⓜ Madeleine

IZRAËL

Colorful souk spilling North African and Middle Eastern goodies onto sidewalk. Sacks of grains, bottles of spices, piles of African baskets.

J6 ✉ 30 rue François Miron 75004 ☎ 01 42 72 66 23 Ⓜ Hôtel de Ville

LEGRAND FILLES ET FILS

Fine wines and selected groceries in a shop dating from 1890. Helpful advice, wide price range but reliable quality. Occasional wine tastings.

G5 ✉ 1 rue de la Banque 75002 ☎ 01 42 60 07 12 Ⓜ Bourse

LE NÔTRE

Chain of shops renowned for their range of gourmet ready prepared dishes, cakes, chocolates, ices, and superior outside catering.

B7 ✉ 44 rue d'Auteuil 75016 ☎ 01 45 24 52 58 Ⓜ Michel-Ange Auteull

LA MAISON DU MIEL

Countless types of honey—chestnut, lavender, pine-tree, acacia—presented in a pretty, tiled interior dating from 1908.

F4 ✉ 24 rue Vignon 75009 ☎ 01 47 42 26 70 Ⓜ Madeleine

A LA MÈRE DE FAMILLE

Original 18th-century grocery shop with shelves laden with imaginatively created chocolates, sweets, jams, and unusual groceries.

H4 ✉ 35 rue du Faubourg, Montmartre 75009 ☎ 01 47 70 83 69 Ⓜ Le Peletier

LABEYRIE

Specializes in products from the Landes. Goose and duck livers, *foie gras*, truffles, and dried mushrooms of all types.

B7 ✉ 11 rue d'Auteuil 75016 ☎ 01 42 24 17 62 Ⓜ Les Halles

TACHON

Unpretentious old-fashioned cheese shop, renowned for its goat, sheep and cow products.

G5 ✉ 38 rue de Richelieu 75001 ☎ 01 42 96 08 66 Ⓜ Palais-Royal/Musée du Louvre

Chocaholics

Chocolate came to Europe via Spain from South America. Under Louis XIV it became a fashionable drink and was served three times a week at Versailles. Paris's first chocolate shop opened in 1659. Voltaire drank up to 12 cups a day, and Napoleon apparently had a penchant for chocolate first thing in the morning. But with their consumption of a mere 12lb. per person per annum, the French lag behind the Swiss, who consume an annual 22lb., and the Belgians at 15lb. Debauve & Gallais is an original wood-paneled 18th-century pharmacy that became a chocolate shop when the medicinal properties of cocoa were discovered (G6 ✉ 30 rue des Saints-Pères 75007 ☎ 01 45 48 54 67 Ⓜ Saint-Germain-des-Prés).

MARKETS

Food markets

Parisians shop daily for their fresh produce and perfectly ripe cheeses. Temporary food markets spring up on boulevards throughout the city on different days of the week (the Bastille Sunday market is particularly enormous), but permanent food markets exist on rue Poncelet (D3), rue Daguerre (G/F8), and on rue de Buci on the Left Bank (G6). All keep provincial lunch hours, so avoid 1–4PM.

CARREAU DU TEMPLE

A covered market specializing in leather goods. Bargain hard and you may pay half the usual price.

🕀 J5 ✉ 2–8 rue Perée 75003 🕐 Tue–Sun 9–noon Ⓜ Temple

MARCHÉ D'ALIGRE

Secondhand clothes, crockery, and bric-a-brac huddle in the middle of a large, low-priced food market.

🕀 K7 ✉ Place d'Aligre 75012 🕐 Tue–Sun 8–1 Ⓜ Ledru Rollin

MARCHÉ DE MONTREUIL

Jeans and jackets start at the Métro. Persevere across the bridge for domestic appliances, carpets, bric-a-brac, and some great secondhand stuff. Morning is best.

🕀 N6 ✉ Avenue de la Porte de Montreuil 75020 🕐 Sat–Mon 7–6 Ⓜ Porte de Montreuil

MARCHÉ AUX OISEAUX

Caged birds whistle and chirp for new owners every Sunday. During the week (except Monday) there is a flower market.

🕀 H6 ✉ Place Louis Lépine 75004 🕐 Sun 9–7 Ⓜ Cité

MARCHÉ AUX PUCES DE SAINT-OUEN

(► 42)

MARCHÉ DE LA RUE LEPIC

Up a steep hill, but worth the effort. Head down the other side of the hill to the rue du Poteau (🕀 G/H2 Ⓜ Jules-Joffrin) for African foods.

🕀 G3 ✉ Rue Lepic 75018 🕐 Tue–Sat 9–1, 4–7; Sun 9–1 Ⓜ Abbesses

MARCHÉ DE LA RUE MONTORGUEIL

A microcosm of what was Les Halles food market (now moved to Rungis in the suburbs), this is a marble-paved pedestrian street with atmosphere and plenty of trendy little bars and lunch places.

🕀 H5 ✉ Rue Montorgueil 75001 🕐 Tue–Sat 9–1, 4–7; Sun 9–1 Ⓜ Les Halles

MARCHÉ DE LA RUE MOUFFETARD

A tourist classic straggling down a winding, narrow, hilly street. Wonderful array of fruit and vegetables, and plenty of aromatic cheeses and charcuterie. Good café stops en route.

🕀 H8 ✉ Rue Mouffetard 75005 🕐 Tue, Thu, Sat 9–1, 4–7 Ⓜ Monge

MARCHÉ AUX TIMBRES

Philatelists zoom in here to buy and sell their miniature treasures.

🕀 E5 ✉ Rond-Point des Champs-Elysées 75008 🕐 Thu, Sat, Sun and holidays 9–7 Ⓜ Franklin D. Roosevelt

MARCHÉ DE VANVES

A favorite with yuppies hot on 1950s and art-deco styles. Secondhand furniture, bric-a-brac, paintings, prints, and some ethnic items.

🕀 E9 ✉ Avenue Georges Lafenestre, Avenue Marc Sangnier 75014 🕐 Sat, Sun 7–7:30 Ⓜ Porte de Vanves

ART & ANTIQUES

ARTCURIAL

Large store of contemporary art (prints, jewelry, sculpture, carpets). An excellent art bookstore is on site.

✚ E4 ✉ 9 avenue Matignon 75008 ☎ 01 42 99 16 16 🕐 Tue–Sat 10:30–7:15 Ⓜ Franklin D. Roosevelt

CARRÉ RIVE GAUCHE

This grid of streets is home to some of Paris's top antique dealers. Archeological pieces, Louis XIV, XV, Empire, Japanese scrolls, 19th-century bronzes, astrolabes, prints—it's all here.

✚ G6 ✉ Rue du Bac, quai Voltaire, rue des Saints-Pères, rue de l'Université 75007 🕐 Tue–Sat 10:30–7 Ⓜ Rue du Bac

GALERIE DOCUMENTS

Original posters and etchings from 1890 to 1940 by such masters as Toulouse-Lautrec and Mucha.

✚ G6 ✉ 53 rue de Seine 75006 ☎ 01 43 54 50 68 🕐 Tue–Sat 10:30–12:30, 2:30–7 Ⓜ Odéon

GALERIE DURAND-DESSERT

Spectacular conversion of an old Bastille mattress factory into a conceptual art mecca.

✚ K6 ✉ 28 rue de Lappe 75011 ☎ 01 48 06 92 23 🕐 Tue–Sat 11–7 Ⓜ Bastille

GALERIE DU JOUR AGNÈS B

Fashion meets art at Agnès B's gallery, with young, hip talent on view in photography and painting.

✚ H5 ✉ 6 rue du Jour 75001 ☎ 01 42 33 43 40 🕐 Tue–Sat 11–7 Ⓜ Les Halles

GALERIE MONTENAY

A longstanding contemporary art gallery, where young French and foreign artists are regularly exhibited.

✚ G6 ✉ 31 rue Mazarine 75006 ☎ 01 43 54 85 30 🕐 Tue–Sat 11–1, 2:30–7 Ⓜ Odéon

LOUVRE DES ANTIQUAIRES

Huge, modernized complex of antique shops. You'll find everything from Eastern carpets to Lalique glass, jewelry, furniture, silver, porcelain, and paintings. High prices.

✚ G5 ✉ 2 place du Palais-Royal 75001 ☎ 01 42 97 27 00 🕐 Tue–Sun 11–7 Ⓜ Palais-Royal/Musée du Louvre

VILLAGE SAINT-PAUL

A cluster of antique and bric-a-brac shops opening onto an enclosed square. Shops continue down the streets on either side, with everything from Asian textiles to glass, old furniture, or clothes.

✚ J6 ✉ Rue Saint-Paul, rue Charlemagne 75004 🕐 Thu–Mon 11–7 Ⓜ Saint-Paul

VILLAGE SUISSE

Network of upscale furniture and antique shops in a chic residential area.

✚ D7 ✉ 54 avenue de la Motte-Piquet, 78 avenue de Suffren 75015 ☎ 01 43 06 69 90 🕐 Thu–Sun 10:30–7 Ⓜ La Motte-Piquet

Galleries

Even if you cannot afford to invest in contemporary art, Paris offers a good window on the latest movements. Art has traditionally centered on the Left Bank around the rue de Seine, but today the more avant-garde galleries spread east from the Centre Georges Pompidou area through the Marais to the Bastille. Pick up a free gallery map at one of the galleries and follow the creative route.

BOOKS & RECORDS

Sunday openings

Sundays now have a strong consumer element to them at the new marble-clad Carrousel du Louvre, perfect for a rainy day. Offerings include a Virgin record/bookstore, a newsagent with a wide international selection, Bodum kitchenware, Nature et Découvertes (a fashionably "ecological" toy and gadget shop), a stylish optician, and various boutiques. The entrance is from 99 rue de Rivoli or by the Carrousel arch in the Louvre.

BRENTANO'S

Well-stocked American bookstore with good travel and art sections at the back. Bilingual staff.
✚ G5 ✉ 37 avenue de l'Opéra 75001 ☎ 01 42 61 52 50 Ⓜ Opéra

LA CHAMBRE CLAIRE

Excellent photography bookstore with a wide range of international publications. Occasional exhibitions.
✚ G7 ✉ 14 rue Saint-Sulpice 75006 ☎ 01 46 34 04 31 🕐 Mon–Sat Ⓜ Odéon

FNAC

The main branch of this firmly established cultural chain. Books, records, cameras, audio, computer accessories. Fair-price policy reigns and staff are helpful.
✚ G7 ✉ 136 rue de Rennes 75006 ☎ 01 49 54 30 00 Ⓜ Saint-Sulpice

GALIGNANI

Pleasantly traditional, spacious bookstore brimming with laden tables and shelves. Large stock of English, German, and French literature and art books.
✚ G5 ✉ 224 rue de Rivoli 75001 ☎ 01 42 60 76 07 Ⓜ Tuileries

LA HUNE

Excellent literary bookstore with extensive art and architecture section. Both French and imported books. Great for late-night browsing—doors open weekdays until midnight.
✚ G6 ✉ 170 boulevard Saint-Germain 75006 ☎ 01 45 48 35 85 Ⓜ Saint-Germain-des-Prés

INSTITUT GÉOGRAPHIQUE NATIONAL

The best map store in Paris with a huge assortment of both French and international maps and guides.
✚ E4 ✉ 107 rue la Boetie 75008 ☎ 01 43 98 85 00 Ⓜ Franklin D. Roosevelt

LIBRAIRIE DES FEMMES

A feminist bookstore with a vast choice of inter-national women writers. Next to the Saint-Germain market.
✚ G7 ✉ 74 rue de Seine 75006 ☎ 01 43 29 50 75 Ⓜ Odéon

LIBRAIRIE GOURMANDE

Cookery and gastronomy titles new and old serve up treats for gourmets.
✚ H6-H7 ✉ 4 rue Dante 75005 ☎ 01 43 54 37 27 Ⓜ Saint-Michel

W H SMITH

Paris branch of one of the UK market leaders, offering a vast selection of English language titles, including books, magazines, and videos.
✚ F5 ✉ 248 rue de Rivoli 75001 ☎ 01 44 77 88 99 Ⓜ Concorde

VIRGIN MEGASTORE

Enormous palace of records with generous opening hours, plus a chic café. Another branch is in the Carrousel du Louvre, 99 rue de Rivoli (✚ G5).
✚ E4 ✉ 52–60 Champs Élysées 75008 ☎ 01 49 53 50 00 🕐 Daily 10AM–midnight; Sun noon–midnight Ⓜ Franklin D. Roosevelt

MISCELLANEOUS

L'ART DU BUREAU
High-tech and designer accessories for the desktop; tasteful stationery.

🔲 J6 ✉ 47 rue des Francs Bourgeois 75004 ☎ 01 48 87 57 97 🚇 Saint-Paul

AXIS
Witty contemporary objects, plates, teapots, jewelry, and clocks. Another shop is at the Bastille, 13 rue de Charonne (🔲 K6).

🔲 G6 ✉ 18 rue Guénégaud 75006 ☎ 01 43 29 66 23 🚇 Odéon

CHRISTIAN TORTU
Anemones, amaryllis, and apple-blossom—this is the place for the ultimate bouquet. Wrapping is in understated brown paper bound with raffia.

🔲 G6 ✉ 6 Carrefour de l'Odéon 75006 ☎ 01 43 26 02 56 🚇 Odéon

CUISINOPHILE
Tiny shop packed with decorative old kitchen utensils, mostly in working order.

🔲 J6 ✉ 28 rue du Bourg Tibourg 75004 ☎ 01 40 29 07 32 🚇 Hôtel de Ville

DEHILLERIN
Food-lover's paradise, brimming with copper pans, knives, bains-marie, sieves, and more. Mail-order service.

🔲 H5 ✉ 18 rue de la Coquillière 75001 ☎ 01 42 36 53 13 🚇 Les Halles

DIPTYQUE
Perfumed candles and *eau de toilette*, plus men's ties, scarves, and superb glasses.

🔲 H7 ✉ 34 boulevard Saint-Germain 75005 ☎ 01 43 26 45 27 🚇 Maubert-Mutualité

IKUO
A tiny shop packed with interesting jewelry, mainly by Japanese creators. Good value.

🔲 G6 ✉ 11 rue des Grands-Augustins 75006 ☎ 01 43 29 56 39 🚇 Pont Neuf

JEAN LAPORTE
An aromatic universe of potpourris, essences, candles, and perfumes based on floral, fruity, and spicy themes.

🔲 F6 ✉ 84 bis rue de Grenelle 75007 ☎ 01 45 44 61 57 🚇 Rue du Bac

NAÏLA DE MONBRISON
Gallery showing some of the most sought-after contemporary jewelry; designers include Marcial Berro, Tina Chow, Mattia Bonetti.

🔲 F6 ✉ 6 rue de Bourgogne 75007 ☎ 01 47 05 11 15 🚇 Varenne

PAPIER +
Emporium of quality paper in endless subtle hues. Superbly bound books, files, and bouquets of colored pencils.

🔲 J6 ✉ 9 rue du Pont Louis-Philippe 75004 ☎ 01 42 77 70 49 🚇 Pont Marie

SI TU VEUX
Charming toy store with affordable and interesting toys, games and dressing-up gear. Separate section devoted to teddy-bear-related items.

🔲 G5 ✉ 68 Galerie Vivienne 75002 ☎ 01 42 60 59 97 🚇 Bourse

Window-shopping
Some Parisian streets do not fit any convenient label and so make for intriguing window-shopping. Try rue Jean-Jacques Rousseau and Passage Véro-Dodat (🔲 G5–H5), rue Saint-Roch (🔲 G5), rue Monsieur-le-Prince and parallel rue de l'Odéon (🔲 G7), rue Saint-Sulpice, rue des Francs-Bourgeois and rue du Pont-Louis-Philippe (🔲 J6), or rue de la Roquette (🔲 K6–L6). For luxury goods take a stroll along the rue du Faubourg-Saint-Honoré (🔲 E4–G5).

Ethnic attractions
Gourmets suffering from a surfeit of delectable but outrageously priced French groceries should head for Paris's ethnic areas. For Indian products the Passage Brady (🔲 H4) is unbeatable, while the nearby rue d'Enghien harbors several Turkish grocery stores. Belleville offers both Arab and Chinese specialties, while the Goutte d'Or (Barbès) focuses on Africa. For a real taste of the Far East, go to the Chinese supermarket Tang Frères at 47 avenue d'Ivry in the 13th *arrondissement* (🔲 J9).

FASHION

Top designers

No trip to Paris would be complete without a stroll down the rue du Faubourg-Saint-Honoré and the even more elegant shopping of the avenue Montaigne. A roll-call of top designers leaves one gaping at the style, and the prices.

AGNÈS B

Pioneering designer who now rests on her comfortable reputation; still a favorite for her unchanging classics. Her shops monopolize most of this street. Children's and men's clothes too.

✚ H5 ✉ 2, 3, 6, 10, 19 rue du Jour 75001 ☎ 01 45 08 56 56 ⓠ Les Halles

ANTHONY PETO

The male answer to Marie Mercié (► 81). Inventive and wearable men's quality headgear from top hats to berets, all aimed at the young and hip.

✚ G5 ✉ 12 rue Jean-Jacques-Rousseau 75001 ☎ 01 42 21 47 15 ⓠ Louvre-Rivoli

AZZEDINE ALAYA

Silhouette-hugging dresses as worn by Tina Turner, Grace Jones and various supermodels. Go to 18 rue de la Verrerie for last season's designs at bargain prices.

✚ H6 ✉ 7 rue de Mousst 75004 ☎ 01 42 72 19 19 ⓠ Hôtel de Ville

BARBARA BUI

One of Paris's most talented young designers. You'll find silky flowing fabrics in subtle colors, well-cut suits, and a superb setting by Pucci de Rossi.

✚ H5 ✉ 23 rue Étienne-Marcel 75001 ☎ 01 40 26 43 65 ⓠ Étienne-Marcel

CHANTAL THOMASS

Paris's sexiest clothes shop, suspiciously reminiscent of an upscale brothel. Stockings, lacy lingerie, and some equally seductive clothes.

✚ G5 ✉ 1 rue Vivienne 75001 ☎ 01 40 15 01 36 ⓠ Bourse

CHÉRI-BIBI

Amusing and inventive women's hats at very affordable prices. Bit of a trek but worth it.

✚ K6 ✉ 82 rue de Charonne 75011 ☎ 01 43 70 51 72 ⓠ Charonne

COLETTE

The place to go for leading design in fashion and home furnishings—from Alexander McQueen to Tom Dixon and the very latest from Sony.

✚ G5 ✉ 213 rue Saint-Honoré 75001 ☎ 01 55 35 33 90 ⓠ Palais-Royal

COMME DES GARÇONS

Two stores of glass and concrete contain Rei Kawakubo's fabrics and androgynous styles.

✚ H5 ✉ 40 & 42 rue Étienne-Marcel 75002 ☎ women 01 42 33 05 21, men 01 42 36 91 54 ⓠ Étienne-Marcel

DIDIER LUDOT

Rare vintage designer clothes (Chanel, Dior, Balmain) and classic Hermès handbags. Picturesque location.

✚ G5 ✉ 24 Galerie Montpensier 75001 ☎ 01 42 96 06 56 ⓠ Palais-Royal, Musée du Louvre

FRANCK ET FILS

Over 100 years old but now reinvented as an elegant boutique with the top names in fashions.

✚ C6 ✉ 80 rue de Passy 75016 ☎ 01 44 14 38 00 ⓠ Passy

GALERIE GAULTIER

One of the most innovative of French designers offers bespoke high fashion and ready-to-wear.

✚ K6 ✉ 30 rue du Faubourg Saint Antoine 75012 ☎ 01 44 68 84 84 Ⓜ Bastille

L'HABILLEUR

Leftover designer stock at huge discounts. Plenty of choice, with helpful sales staff.

✚ J5 ✉ 44 rue de Poitou 75003 ☎ 01 48 87 77 12 Ⓜ Saint-Sébastien-Froissart

IRIÉ

A former Kenzo assistant creates superbly cut and accessibly priced separates. A pioneer on this discreet street.

✚ G6 ✉ 8 rue du Pré-aux-Clercs 75007 ☎ 01 42 61 18 28 Ⓜ Rue du Bac

KOOKAI

Flagship store of this fun, trendy chain, popular with the young.

✚ C5 ✉ 12 rue Gustave-Courbet 75016 ☎ 01 47 55 18 00 Ⓜ Victor Hugo

LOLITA LEMPICKA

Established inventive chic, very Parisienne. Ultra-feminine details and shop design.

✚ F5 ✉ 14 rue du Faubourg-Saint-Honoré 75008 ☎ 01 49 24 94 01 Ⓜ Concorde

MARIE MERCIÉ

Extravagant hats. Choose your headgear here or in her original shop near Les Halles at 56 rue Tiquetonne (✚ H5).

✚ G7 ✉ 23 rue Saint-Sulpice 75006 ☎ 01 43 26 45 83 Ⓜ Odéon

MI-PRIX

Designer clothes at a fraction of the price; also shoes by Michel Perry.

✚ C8 ✉ 27 boulevard Victor 75015 ☎ 01 48 28 42 48 Ⓜ Porte de Versailles

MOUTON À CINQ PATTES

Cut-price designer clothes packeds into a crowded shop. Another branch is at 15 rue Vieille du Temple (✚ J6).

✚ G6 ✉ 19 rue Grégoire des Tours 75006 ☎ 01 43 29 73 56 Ⓜ Odéon

SCOOTER

To get that real Les Halles look, drop in here for the latest accessories: ethnic, 1960s/70s revival transformed into jewelry, bags, and clothes.

✚ H5 ✉ 10 rue de Turbigo 75001 ☎ 01 45 08 89 31 Ⓜ Les Halles

SONIA RYKIEL

Ready-to-wear fashion house with economy range of accessories and cosmetics. Menswear is across the road.

✚ G6 ✉ 175 boulevard Saint-Germain 75006 ☎ 01 49 54 60 60 Ⓜ Saint-Germain-des-Prés

SOULEIADO

Cheerful range of fabrics, table linen, and cushions in bright Provençal prints.

✚ G6 ✉ 78 rue de Seine 75006 ☎ 01 43 54 62 25 Ⓜ Mabillon

VICTOIRE

Cool salon for hot fashions with less-expensive own-label clothes next door.

✚ G5–H5 ✉ 12 place des Victoires 75002 ☎ 01 42 61 09 02 Ⓜ Bourse/Palais-Royal

Fashion hubs

The fact that women's high fashion is concentrated in just three centers makes clothes shopping, or mere window-gazing, easy. The hub of place des Victoires (home to Kenzo, Stephane Kélian, Plein Sud, and Victoire) continues along the rue Étienne-Marcel and toward Les Halles. The Marais's enticing offerings run between the rue de Sévigné, rue des Rosiers, place des Vosges, and side streets. Saint-Germain burgeons along and off the boulevard, rue de Grenelle, and continues up the boulevard Raspail.

Zen cuts

Issey Miyake reigns OK! His sculptural, finely pleated creations in imaginative synthetics are sold at 3 Place des Vosges 75004 (☎ 01 48 87 01 86), but Plantation/Issey Miyake at 17 Boulevard Raspail 75007 (☎ 01 45 48 12 32) is where more accessible designs are available. If black and white is your style, head for Yohji Yamamoto at 25 rue du Louvre 75001 (☎ 01 42 21 42 93) for sober geometric cuts for men and women.

81

CONCERTS, JAZZ CLUBS & NIGHTCLUBS

Inexpensive concerts

Numerous classical music concerts are held in churches—try Saint-Eustache, Saint-Germain-des-Prés, Saint-Julien-le-Pauvre, Saint-Louis-en-l'Île, Saint-Roch, and Saint-Séverin. Seats are reasonably priced and the quality of music is sometimes very high. In May–September free concerts are held in parks all over the city. Programs are available at the Office du Tourisme or the Hôtel de Ville, or ☎ 01 40 71 76 47.

Recitals

Chopin gave his last recital at what is now the most prestigious venue on the classical circuit and home to the Orchestre de Paris—the Salle Pleyel (✉ 252 rue du Faubourg-Saint-Honoré ☎ 01 45 61 53 00). It is the venue for many of Paris's major concerts, often with world-famous soloists, and for recordings. Another established concert hall, the Salle Gaveau, still attracts top international opera singers and pianists despite its shabby appearance (✉ 45 rue de la Boétie 75008 ☎ 01 49 53 05 07).

CONCERT VENUES

AUDITORIUM DES HALLES
Lunchtime and early evening concerts and recitals: classical music, world music, jazz.
➕ H5 ✉ Forum des Halles, Porte Sainte-Eustache 75001 ☎ 01 42 36 13 90 🚇 Les Halles

CITÉ DE LA MUSIQUE
Accessible classical, jazz, and world music at this new concert hall in an out-of-the-way location.
➕ L2 ✉ 221 avenue Jean-Jaurès 75019 ☎ 01 44 84 44 84 🚇 Porte de Pantin

OPÉRA BASTILLE
Long-term teething problems continue at Paris's "people's" opera house. Opera, recitals, dance, and even theater.
➕ K6 ✉ 120 rue de Lyon 75012 ☎ 01 43 43 96 96 🚇 Bastille

OPÉRA COMIQUE
Sumptuously decorated opera house that stages light opera, dance, and sometimes theater.
➕ G4 ✉ 5 rue Favart 75002 ☎ 01 42 44 45 46 🚇 Richelieu-Drouot

THÉÂTRE DES CHAMPS-ÉLYSÉES
Top international orchestras play in a stately setting. Expensive.
➕ E5 ✉ 15 avenue Montaigne 75008 ☎ 01 49 52 50 00 🚇 Alma-Marceau

THÉÂTRE DU CHÂTELET
Varied program of opera, symphonic music, and dance. Cheap seats for lunchtime.
➕ H6 ✉ place du Châtelet 75001 ☎ 01 40 28 28 40 🚇 Châtelet

THÉÂTRE DE LA VILLE
Modern theater with an adventurous program of contemporary dance, avant-garde music, theater, and early evening recitals of world music.
➕ H6 ✉ Place du Châtelet 75004 ☎ 01 42 74 22 77 🚇 Châtelet

JAZZ CLUBS

BILBOQUET
Traditional jazz, pricey cocktails, and a strait-laced crowd with a good sprinkling of tourists. Restaurant.
➕ G6 ✉ 13 rue Saint-Benoît 75006 ☎ 01 45 48 81 84 🚇 Saint-Germain-des-Prés

CAVEAU DE LA HUCHETTE
Still going strong, a smoky basement bar with dancing and live jazz from 9:30PM.
➕ H6 ✉ 5 rue de la Huchette 75005 ☎ 01 43 26 65 05 🚇 Saint-Michel

CHAPELLE DES LOMBARDS
Funky Bastille haunt with a hot atmosphere. Caribbean, raï (Algerian rock), and rap music. Open until dawn.
➕ K6 ✉ 19 rue de Lappe 75011 ☎ 01 43 57 24 24 🕐 Thu–Sat 🚇 Bastille

NEW MORNING
One of Paris's top jazz/blues/soul bars. Good

atmosphere, dedicated crowd. Reserve for top names.

⊞ H4 ✉ 7/9 rue des Petites-Écuries 75010 ☎ 01 45 23 51 41 🚇 Château d'Eau

PETIT OPPORTUN
Classic jazz venue in Les Halles featuring live bands from 10:30PM. Reasonable prices.

⊞ H6 ✉ 15 rue des Lavandières-Sainte-Opportun 75001 ☎ 01 42 36 01 36 ⏰ Closed Sun 🚇 Châtelet

LE SUNSET
Part of the Les Halles cluster, a restaurant-bar with good jazz from 10PM until the small hours. Reasonably priced food.

⊞ H6 ✉ 60 rue des Lombards 75001 ☎ 01 40 26 46 60 🚇 Châtelet

LA VILLA
Top jazz names. Sleek cocktail bar in stylish post-modern hotel basement, open late. Reserve.

⊞ G6 ✉ 29 rue Jacob 75006 ☎ 01 43 26 60 00 ⏰ Closed Sun 🚇 Saint-Germain-des-Prés

NIGHTCLUBS

L'ARC
Fairly upscale club with selective door policy. Piano bar, restaurant, and indoor garden.

⊞ D4 ✉ 12 rue de Presbourg, 75016 ☎ 01 45 00 45 00 ⏰ Nightly from 11:30PM 🚇 Charles de Gaulle-Étoile

LES BAINS
Still number one for the fashion and showbiz set. Heavy door policing—go very late. Restaurant.

⊞ H5 ✉ 7 rue du Bourg-l'Abbé 75003 ☎ 01 48 87 01 80 ⏰ Nightly 🚇 Étienne-Marcel

LE BALAJO
Over 60 years old with ritzy 1930s decor. The music is mainly disco, techno, and funk.

⊞ K6 ✉ 9 rue de Lappe 75011 ☎ 01 47 00 07 87 ⏰ Thu–Sat 🚇 Bastille

LE BATACLAN
An old favorite now rejuvenated. You'll find the fashion-media set, with fancy dress on Fridays, mainly house music on Saturdays.

⊞ K5 ✉ 50 boulevard Voltaire 75011 ☎ 01 44 00 39 12 ⏰ Thu–Sat from 11PM 🚇 Oberkampf

PIGALL'S
Latest Pigalle haunt that thunders soul, acid-jazz. Transvestites add to the funkiness.

⊞ G3 ✉ 77 rue Pigalle 75009 ☎ 01 46 27 82 82 ⏰ Thu–Sat from 12PM 🚇 Pigalle

RÉGINE
Flashy mature crowd, rich in media stars. Careful grooming matters, so look neat—you may be lucky.

⊞ E4 ✉ 49–51 rue de Ponthieu 75008 ☎ 01 43 59 21 13 🚇 Franklin D. Roosevelt

LE TANGO
Unpretentious club with Afro-Latino rhythms, tango, salsa, reggae, and soul.

⊞ J5 ✉ 13 rue au Maire 75003 ☎ 01 42 72 17 78 ⏰ Fri–Sat from 11PM 🚇 Arts et Métiers

Clubs and raves

Paris clubbing is both serious and fickle—serious because no truly cool Parisian turns up before midnight, and fickle because mass loyalties change rapidly. Most clubs keep going through the night until dawn on Friday and Saturday nights, and nearly all charge an entry (this usually includes a drink). For impromptu raves, theme nights, and house parties outside Paris, with shuttles provided, check *Pariscope*'s English section or key in to Minitel 3615 Party News.

BARS & SPECIAL FILM THEATERS

Cinephile's paradise

Though French film production dropped below the 100 mark in 1994, the capital is still a cinephile's paradise. With some 350 movies shown each day, the choice can be tantalizing. Foreign movies shown in their original languages have "*VO*" (*version originale*) after the title. New movies come out on Wednesdays, which is also the day for all-round reductions. The Gaumont and UGC cinemas offer multiple-entry cards that can be used for up to three people and save precious francs.

BARS

BAR DU MARCHÉ
A hip watering hole with good sounds and cheerful service. Nice outdoor terrace.
G6 ⊠ 75 rue de Seine 75006 ☎ 01 43 26 55 15
Daily 8AM–1AM
Odéon

BAR ROMAIN
Original 1905 decor brightens this bar-restaurant, popular with a more mature showbiz crowd. Choice of over 200 cocktails.
G4 ⊠ 6 rue de Caumartin 75009 ☎ 01 47 42 98 04
Mon–Sat midnight–2AM
Havre-Caumartin

BIRDLAND
An old Saint-Germain favorite. Relaxed atmosphere, with great jazz records.
G6 ⊠ 8 rue Princesse 75006 ☎ 01 43 26 97 59
Nightly 7PM–6AM
Mabillon

LES BOUCHONS
Late-night basement bar with occasional live jazz. Cheerful restaurant upstairs.
H6 ⊠ 19 rue des Halles 75001 ☎ 01 42 33 28 73
Nightly 11:30PM–dawn
Châtelet

CAFÉ CANNIBALE
World music in a restored baroque setting in a burgeoning neighborhood near Belleville. Relaxed, spacious, and popular.
K5 ⊠ 93 rue Jean-Pierre-Timbaud 75011 ☎ 01 49 29 95 59 Daily
Couronnes

CAFÉ CHARBON
Hip café-bar with a mirrored interior. Enjoy the budget snacks or read the papers here until 2AM.
K5 ⊠ 109 rue Oberkampf 75011 ☎ 01 43 57 55 13
Daily Ménilmontant

CAFÉ NOIR
Packed, late-night haunt on fringe of Les Halles. High-decibel rock and an unmistakable technicolor exterior.
H5 ⊠ 65 rue Montmartre 75002 ☎ 01 40 39 07 36
Daily 7:30AM–2AM. Closed Sun Sentier

LA CASBAH
Moorish-style bar with dancing, fancily dressed bar staff, great cocktails and decor. Very unfriendly bouncers.
K7 ⊠ 18 rue de la Forge-Royale 75011 ☎ 01 43 71 71 89 Wed–Sat 11:30PM onwards Faidherbe-Chaligny

CHINA CLUB
Hip and crowded red-lacquered bar-restaurant peopled by Mao-style waiters. Avoid the food, go for a drink. Another bar upstairs.
K7 ⊠ 50 rue de Charenton 75012 ☎ 01 43 43 82 02
Nightly 7PM–2AM
Ledru Rollin, Bastille

HARRY'S BAR
Old pub atmosphere. Rowdy, mature, well-tanked-up crowd.
G5 ⊠ 5 rue Daunou 75002 ☎ 01 42 61 71 14 Nightly 10:30PM–4AM Opéra

JACQUES MÉLAC
Inexpensive French wines by the glass or bottled for

you from the barrel.
✚ L6 ✉ 42 rue Léon Frot
75011 ☎ 01 43 70 59 27
🕐 Closed Sat, Sun and mid-Jul
to mid-Aug Ⓜ Charonne

MAYFLOWER
Lively, reasonably priced
bar-pub that has attracted
student nighthawks for
years.
✚ H7 ✉ 49 rue Descartes
75005 ☎ 01 43 54 56 47
🕐 Daily 7AM–2AM Ⓜ Cardinal
Lemoine

LE MOLOKO
Cavernous, popular bar on
two floors. Loud—but you
can still talk.
✚ G3 ✉ 26 rue Fontaine
75009 ☎ 01 48 74 50 26
🕐 Daily 9:30PM–6AM
Ⓜ Blanche

LA TARTINE
An old daytime classic.
French wines by the glass,
cold platters of
charcuterie, and cheese.
✚ J6 ✉ 24 rue de Rivoli
75004 ☎ 01 42 72 76 85
🕐 8:30AM–10PM. Closed Tue,
Aug Ⓜ Hôtel de Ville

LE TRAIN BLEU
Striking belle-époque
setting that functions as a
restaurant-bar. The food is
pricey; stick to drinks.
✚ K7 ✉ 1st floor, Gare de
Lyon 75012 ☎ 01 43 43
09 06 🕐 Daily 9AM–11PM
Ⓜ Gare de Lyon

WEB BAR
Funky little cyber café
that provides art shows,
videos, and music daily
until 2AM. Good weekend
brunches.
✚ J5 ✉ 32 rue de Picardie
75003 ☎ 01 42 72 57 47
🕐 Daily Ⓜ République

SPECIAL FILM THEATERS

LA CINÉMATHÈQUE FRANÇAISE
Cinema classics, with
foreign movies always in
the original language.
✚ H4 ✉ 42 boulevard Bonne-
Nouvelle 75010 ☎ 01 47 04
24 24 Ⓜ Bonne-Nouvelle

LE DÔME IMAX
The world's largest
hemispherical screen
(12,314 square feet).
Digital sound system.
✚ Off map at A2 ✉ 1 place
du Dôme, La Défense 92905
☎ 01 46 92 45 45 Ⓜ La
Défense

L'ENTREPOT
Stimulating program of
French and foreign
movies, plus festivals
devoted to one director.
Bookstore, pleasant café.
✚ F8 ✉ 7–9 rue Francis-de-
Pressensé 75014 ☎ 01 45 43
41 63 Ⓜ Pernéty

LA PAGODE
A unique film theater
housed inside an exotic
Japanese pagoda.
Adjoining tea room
and garden.
✚ F6 ✉ 57 bis rue de
Babylone 75007 ☎ 01 45 55
48 48 Ⓜ Saint-François Xavier

VIDÉOTHÈQUE DE PARIS
Movies or documentaries
shot in or connected with
Paris, and film classics. A
cheap day pass admits you
to four different movies.
✚ H5 ✉ Grand Galerie,
Forum des Halles, Porte Sainte-
Eustache 75001 ☎ 01 44 76
62 00 Ⓜ Les Halles

Steambaths
If nocturnal bar-crawling
becomes too much, why not
sweat it out at a steambath? The
hammam at the Mosquée
(➤ 52) offers a lovely tiled
interior à la Marrakesh
(🕐 Men: Fri, Sun. Women:
Mon, Wed, Thu, Sat). A new
though pricier alternative is Les
Bains du Marais (✉ 31 rue des
Blancs-Manteaux 75004 ☎ 01
44 61 02 02 🕐 Men: Thu, Sat.
Women: Mon–Wed).

SPORTS

Pools and horses

Paris's municipal swimming pools have complicated opening hours that are largely geared to schoolchildren. Phone beforehand to check for public hours and avoid Wednesdays and Saturdays, both favorites with children off school. Gymnase Clubs are generally open until 9PM but close on Sundays. If horse-racing is your passion, don't miss the harness racing at Vincennes with its brilliant flashes of color-coordinated horses and jockeys. Check *Paris-Turf* for race programs.

AQUABOULEVARD
Huge family complex with water-shoots, palm trees, Jacuzzis. Gym, putting greens, tennis and squash courts too—at a price.
✚ C8 ✉ 4–6 rue Louis Armand 75015 ☎ 01 40 60 10 00 Ⓜ Balard

GYMNASE CLUB
Best-equipped gymnasium in this chain. ☎ 01 44 37 24 24 for details on other gyms throughout Paris. Day passes, book of ten passes, or annual subscription.
✚ D3 ✉ 17 rue du Débarcadère 75017 ☎ 01 45 74 14 04 Ⓜ Porte Maillot

HIPPODROME D'AUTEUIL
Flat-racing and hurdles. Hosts the prestigious Prix du Président de la République hurdle race.
✚ A6 ✉ Bois de Boulogne, 75016 ☎ 01 44 10 20 30 Ⓒ Closed Jul, Aug Ⓜ Porte d'Auteuil

HIPPODROME DE LONGCHAMP
Longchamp is where the hats and champagne come out for the annual Prix de l'Arc de Triomphe. Regular flat-races.
✚ Off map at A6 ✉ Bois de Boulogne 75016 ☎ 01 44 30 75 00 Ⓒ Closed Jul, Aug Ⓜ Porte d'Auteuil, then free bus

HIPPODROME DE VINCENNES
Colorful harness racing pulls in the crowds. Watch out for the Prix d'Amérique, the top harness race of the season.
✚ Off map at N9 ✉ 2 route de la Ferme, Bois de Vincennes 75012 ☎ 01 49 77 17 17

Ⓒ Closed Jul, Aug Ⓜ Château de Vincennes, then shuttle

PARC DES PRINCES
Huge municipal stadium takes 50,000 spectators for major domestic soccer and rugby games. Home to Paris Saint-Germain F.C.
✚ A8 ✉ 24 rue du Commandant-Guilbaud 75016 ☎ 01 49 87 29 29 Ⓜ Porte d'Auteuil

PISCINE DES HALLES (SUZANNE BERLIOUX)
Underground 50m pool overlooked by lush tropical garden.
✚ H5 ✉ 10 place de la Rotonde 75001 ☎ 01 42 36 98 44 Ⓜ Les Halles

PISCINE JEAN TARIS
Two 25m pools with view of Panthéon. Electronically cleaned water, so no chlorine.
✚ H7 ✉ 16 rue Thouin 75005 ☎ 01 43 25 54 03 Ⓜ Mange

STADE DE FRANCE
Splendid new home of international soccer as witnessed by the successful hosting of World Cup '98.
✚ J1 ✉ rue Francis-de-Pressensé 93210 Saint Denis ☎ 01 55 93 00 00 Ⓡ RER Saint Denis

ROLAND-GARROS
Clay-court home to the French Tennis Open. Tickets are sold months ahead but plenty of racketeers sell seats on the day at the main entrance.
✚ A7 ✉ 2 avenue Gordon-Bennett 75016 ☎ 01 47 43 48 00 Ⓜ Porte d'Auteuil, then walk or catch bus 32, 52, 123

PARIS
travel facts

Arriving & Departing	88
Essential Facts	89
Public Transportation	90
Media & Communications	91
Emergencies	92
Language	93

AVENUE
DES
CHAMPS ÉLYSÉES

ARRIVING & DEPARTING

Before you go
- Visas are not required for US or Canadian citizens, or EU nationals, but are obligatory for Australians and New Zealanders.
- Anyone entering France must have a valid passport (or official identity card for EU nationals).
- There are no vaccination requirements.

When to go
- Spring rarely starts before mid-May; June is always glorious.
- July and August see the Great Parisian Exodus. Cultural activities move into bottom gear, but lodging is easier.
- Avoid mid-September to mid-October, the peak trade-fair period, when hotels are full.
- Winter temperatures rarely drop below freezing but rain is usual in January and March.

Arriving by train
- The Eurostar train service from London arrives at Gare du Nord ☎ 08 36 35 35 39
- Trains arrive at the Gare de l'Est from Alsace, Champagne, and Germany.
- The Gare de Lyon serves southeast France and Italy, the Gare d'Austerlitz central southwest France, and Spain.
- The central TGV stations are Gare Montparnasse and Gare de Lyon.
- All stations have Métro, bus, and taxi services.
- For reservations and information on SNCF stations ☎ 01 53 90 20 20 (daily 7AM–9PM)

Arriving by air
- Air passengers arrive either at Roissy-Charles de Gaulle airport (14 miles north of Paris) or at Orly (9 miles to the south).
- Taxis charge a surcharge at airports and at stations, and also for each item of luggage carried.

Roissy
- Connections to downtown are: via a direct RER train into Châtelet-Les Halles; the Air France bus that stops at Étoile (Arc de Triomphe) and Porte Maillot; the cheaper Roissybus that terminates at rue Scribe, Opéra.
- The Air France bus and Roissybus run every 15–20 minutes, 5:40AM–11PM.
- Taxis are expensive.
- For passenger information ☎ 01 48 04 18 24

Orly
- Connections to downtown are via the Air France bus that goes to Invalides every 12 minutes and stops at Porte d'Orléans, or the more economical Orlybus that goes to Denfert-Rochereau every 15 minutes.
- Avoid Orlyrail as this involves a shuttle bus.
- For passenger information ☎ 01 49 75 15 15

Customs regulations
- There are no restrictions on goods brought into France by EU citizens.
- For non-EU nationals the limits are:
  200 cigarettes or 100 cigarillos or 50 cigars or 250g of tobacco; 2 liters of wine; 1 liter of spirits; 50g of perfume; 500g of coffee; and 200g of tea.
- Prescribed medicines and up to 50,000FF of currency may be imported.

Departing

- Airport tax for departing passengers is included in the price of your ticket.
- There are numerous tourist shops at Orly and Roissy airports, but not on Eurostar or other international trains.
- Allow one hour to reach Roissy airport, by any transport means, and 45 minutes for Orly.

ESSENTIAL FACTS

Travel insurance

- Insurance to cover theft, illness, and repatriation is strongly advised.

Opening hours

- Banks: Mon–Fri 9–12, 2–4. Closed on public holidays and often the preceding afternoon.
- Post offices: Mon–Fri 8–7; Sat 8–noon. The central post office (✉ 52 rue du Louvre 75001 ☎ 01 40 28 20 00) provides a 24-hour service for post, telegrams, and telephone.
- Shops: Mon–Sat 9–7 or 10–8. Some close Monday and an hour at lunch. Many close during August. Arab-owned groceries stay open until 9 or 10PM daily.
- Museums: national museums close on Tuesday, municipal museums on Monday. Individual opening hours vary considerably; always phone to check hours for national holidays.

National holidays

- January 1, May 1, May 8, Ascension (last Thursday in May), Whit Monday (early June), July 14, August 15, November 1, November 11, December 25.
- Sunday services for public transportation operate; many restaurants, large shops, and local groceries disregard national holidays.

Money matters

- The French currency is the franc (FF): 1FF = 100 centimes.
- On January 1, 1999, the euro became the official currency of France, and the French franc became a denomination of the euro. French franc notes and coins continue to be legal tender during a transitional period. Euro bank notes and coins are likely to start to be introduced by January 1, 2002.

Foreign exchange

- Only banks with *change* signs change foreign currency/traveler's checks; a passport is necessary. Bureaus de change are open longer hours but rates can be poorer.
- Airport and station exchange desks are open 6:30AM–11PM.
- For late-night exchange in central Paris use Chequepoint ✉ 150 avenue des Champs-Élysées 75008 ☎ 01 49 53 02 51 🕐 24 hours 🚇 Charles de Gaulle-Étoile.

Credit cards

- Credit cards are widely accepted.
- VISA cards (including MasterCard and Diners Club) can be used in cash dispensers. Most machines flash up instructions in the language you choose.
- American Express is less common, so Amex cardholders needing cash should use American Express ✉ 11 rue Scribe 75009 ☎ 01 47 77 70 00 🚇 Opéra.

Etiquette

- Shake hands on introduction and on leaving; once you know people better replace this with a peck on both cheeks.

- Always use *vous* unless the other person breaks into *tu*.
- It is polite to add *Monsieur*, *Madame*, or *Mademoiselle* when addressing strangers or salespeople.
- Always say hello and goodbye in stores.
- When calling waiters, use *Monsieur* or *Madame* (not *garçon*).
- Dress carefully. More emphasis is put on grooming than in other countries.

Women travelers
- Women are safe to travel alone or together. Deal with any unwanted attention firmly and politely.

Places of worship
- The International Center for Religious Information (✉ 6 Place du Parvis-Notre-Dame 75004 ☎ 01 56 56 44 00 Ⓜ Saint-Michel), an English-speaking service, supplies information on services and churches for Catholic, Protestant, and Orthodox worshippers.
- Protestant churches: American Church ✉ 65 Quai d'Orsay 75007 ☎ 01 40 62 05 00 Ⓜ Invalides. St. George's English Church ✉ 7 rue Auguste Vacquerie 75016 ☎ 01 47 20 22 51 Ⓜ Charles de Gaulle-Étoile.
- Jewish: Synagogue ✉ 10 rue Pavée 75004 ☎ 01 42 77 81 51 Ⓜ Saint-Paul.
- Russian Orthodox: Saint Alexandre de la Néva ✉ 12 rue Daru 75008 ☎ 01 42 27 37 34 Ⓜ Courcelles.

Student travelers
- An International Student Identity Card reduces film theater charges, entrance to museums, and air and rail travel.
- AJF (Accueil des Jeunes en

France) ✉ 119 rue Saint-Martin 75004 ☎ 01 42 77 87 80 Ⓜ Châtelet Ⓞ Mon–Sat 9–6:30. Gives advice on hostel accommodations, and discounts on train tickets.
- CIDJ (Centre d'Information et de Documentation Jeunesse) ✉ 101 Quai Branly 75015 ☎ 01 44 49 12 00 Ⓜ Bir-Hakeim Ⓞ Mon–Fri 10–6. Youth information center for jobs, courses, sports.

Time differences
- France is six hours ahead of New York. Clocks change at the autumn and spring solstices.

Toilets
- Public toilet booths are common, and are generally well maintained.
- Every café has a toilet ("Les toilettes, s'il vous plaît?") although standards vary. Do not use a cafe's toilet without ordering at least a drink.

Electricity
- Voltage is 220V and sockets take two round pins.

Tourist Information Office
- Office de Tourisme de Paris ✉ 127 avenue des Champs-Élysées 75008 ☎ 08 36 68 31 12 Ⓞ 9AM–8PM Ⓜ Charles de Gaulle-Étoile. Masses of tourist information and polyglot staff.

PUBLIC TRANSPORTATION

Métro
- Métro lines are identified by their terminus (*direction*) and a number; connections are indicated with orange panels marked *correspondances* on the platform.

- Blue *sortie* signs show the exits.
- The first Métros run at 5:30AM, and the last around 12:30AM.
- Keep your ticket until you exit— it has to be re-slotted on the RER, and ticket inspectors prowl the Métro.
- Avoid rush hours: 8–9:30AM and 4:30–7PM.

Bus

- Hail buses from bus stops.
- Enter, and punch your ticket into the machine beside the driver or flash your pass (see below).
- Night buses run hourly 1:30AM–5:30PM from place du Châtelet out to the *portes* and suburbs.

Tickets and passes

- Tickets and passes function for Métro, buses, and RER.
- Pass prices and the number of tickets required for a ride depend on how many of five travel zones you intend to pass through.
- A *carnet* of ten tickets is considerably cheaper than individual tickets.
- *Mobilis* is a one-day pass, valid on Métro, buses, and RER.
- A *Paris Visite* card gives unlimited travel for three or five days plus discounts at certain monuments.
- The *carte hebdomadaire* pass (photo required) is valid Mon–Sun.
- The *carte orange* pass, also needing a photo, is valid for one calendar month.

Maps

- Free Métro/bus/RER maps are available at every station and on some buses.
- RATP information (in French) ☎ 01 43 46 14 14 ☎ 6AM–9PM.
- RATP tourist office ✉ 53 bis quai des Grands Augustins 75006 ☎ 08 36 68 41 14

Taxis

- Taxis can be hailed in the street if the roof sign is illuminated, or they can be found at ranks.
- Sunday and night rates (7PM–7AM) rise considerably and extra charges are made at stations and Air France terminals for luggage, and for animals.
- Taxi-drivers expect tips of 10 percent.
- Radio-taxi firms: Taxis Bleus (☎ 01 49 36 10 10); Alpha (☎ 01 45 85 85 85); G7 (☎ 01 47 39 47 39); Artaxi (☎ 01 42 41 50 50)

MEDIA & COMMUNICATIONS

Telephones

- Most Parisian phone booths use France Telecom phone cards (*télécarte* for 50 or 120 units), available from post offices, *tabacs*, stations, or at main Métro stations. A few booths still use coins, particularly those in cafés.
- Cheap periods for international calls vary: for the USA and Canada, daily 2AM–noon, with lesser reductions 8PM–2AM; for Europe, Australia, and New Zealand Mon–Sat 9:30PM–8AM and all day Sun.
- Repairs ☎ 13
- Information ☎ 12
- International information ☎ 00 33 12 + country prefix.
- 00 is the prefix for international calls.
- All French telephone numbers have ten digits.
- All numbers in the Île-de-France, including Paris, start with 01 unless at extra rates, when they start with 08.
- To call the French provinces, use: 02 Northwest, 03 Northeast, 04 Southeast, 05 Southwest.

Post offices

- Stamps can be bought at *tabacs*, and mail posted in any yellow mailbox.
- All post offices have free access to the Minitel directory service, express courier post (Chronopost), phone booths, and photocopying machines.

Press

- The main dailies are *Le Monde* (serious center-left), *Libération* (left-wing), and *Le Figaro* (right-wing).
- Weekly news magazines range from the left-wing *Le Nouvel Observateur*, *L'Express* (center) and *Le Point* (center-right) to *Paris Match* and *Canard Enchaîné*. For weekly listings of cultural events, buy a copy of *Pariscope* (with an English section) or *L'Officiel des Spectacles*.
- Central newspaper kiosks and newsagents stock European dailies.
- The NMPP's central bookstore (✉ 93 rue Montmartre 75002) has a range of French and foreign press, while the newsagent in the Carrousel beneath the Louvre carries American press and international fashion publications.

Radio and television

- FM stations run the gamut from current affairs on France Inter (87.8 MHz) to unadulterated rap/rock/house music on Radio Nova (101.5 MHz).
- France 2 and FR3, the state TV channels, occasionally have good documentaries and current events programs. TF1 has lightweight entertainment, and M6 is still evolving. Arte (on Channel 5) is a serious cultural and educational channel. Canal is a popular subscription channel.

EMERGENCIES

Precautions

- Watch wallets and handbags as pickpockets are active, particularly in crowded bars, flea markets, and movie theaters.
- Keep travelers'-check numbers separate from the checks themselves.
- Make a declaration at a local *commissariat* (police station) to claim losses on your insurance.

Lost property

- The police lost-property office is ✉ 36 rue des Morillons 75015 ☎ 01 55 76 20 20 🕒 8:30AM–5PM 🚇 Convention.

Medicines and medical treatment

- Minor ailments can often be treated at pharmacies (identified by a green cross), where staff will also advise on local doctors.
- All public hospitals have a 24-hour emergency service (*urgences*) as well as specialist doctors. Payment is made on the spot, but if you are hospitalized ask to see the *assistante sociale* to arrange payment directly through your insurance.
- House calls are made with SOS Médecins ☎ 01 47 07 77 77, or for dental problems SOS Dentaire ☎ 01 43 37 51 00
- 24-hour pharmacy: Dhéry ✉ 84 avenue des Champs-Élysées 75008 ☎ 01 45 62 02 41
- The Drug-store chain at Opéra and Champs Élysées offers pharmacies, newsagents, cafés, and tobacconists open until 2AM.

Emergency phone numbers

- Crisis-line in English: SOS Help ☎ 01 47 23 80 80 🕒 3–11PM.
- Police ☎ 17

- Ambulance (SAMU) ☎ 15
- Fire (*sapeurs pompiers*) ☎ 18
- Anti-poison ☎ 01 40 37 04 04

Embassies and consulates

- US Embassy ✉ 2 avenue Gabriel 75008 ☎ 01 43 12 22 22 Ⓜ Concorde.
- US Consulate ✉ 2 rue Saint-Florentin 75001 ☎ 01 43 12 22 22.
- Canadian Embassy ✉ 35 avenue Montaigne 75008 ☎ 01 44 33 29 00.
- Canadian Consulate ✉ 37 avenue Montaigne 75008 ☎ 01 44 43 29 16 Ⓜ Franklin D. Roosevelt.
- British Embassy ✉ 35 rue du Faubourg-Saint-Honoré 75008 ☎ 01 44 51 31 00 Ⓜ Concorde.
- British Consulate ✉ 9 avenue Hoche 75008 ☎ 01 44 51 33 01/3 Ⓜ Concorde.
- Australian Embassy ✉ 4 rue Jean-Rey 75015 ☎ 01 40 59 33 00 Ⓜ Bir-Hakeim.
- New Zealand Embassy ✉ 7ter rue Léonard-de-Vinci 75016 ☎ 01 45 00 24 11 Ⓜ Victor Hugo.

LANGUAGE

1	un	16	seize
2	deux	17	dix-sept
3	trois	18	dix-huit
4	quatre	19	dix-neuf
5	cinq	20	vingt
6	six	21	vingt-et-un
7	sept	30	trente
8	huit	40	quarante
9	neuf	50	cinquante
10	dix	60	soixante
11	onze	70	soixante-dix
12	douze	80	quatre-vingts
13	treize	90	quatre-vingt-dix
14	quatorze	100	cent
15	quinze	1,000	mille

Basic vocabulary

yes/no oui/ non
please s'il vous plaît

thank you merci
excuse me excusez-moi
hello bonjour
good evening bon soir
goodbye au revoir
how are you? comment allez-vous? ça va?
very well thanks trés bien merci
how much? combien?
do you speak English? parlez-vous anglais?
I don't understand je ne comprends pas
where is/are…? où est/sont…?
here/there ici/là
turn left/right tournez à gauche/droite
straight on tout droit
behind/in front derrière/devant
when? quand?
today aujourd'hui
yesterday hier
tomorrow demain
how long? combien de temps?
at what time? à quelle heure?
what time do you open/close? à quelle heure ouvrez/ fermez-vous?
do you have…? avez-vous…?
a single room une chambre simple
a double room une chambre double
an extra bed un lit supplementaire
with/without bathroom avec/sans salle de bains
breakfast le petit déjeuner
lunch le déjeuner
dinner le dîner
how much is this? c'est combien?
it's expensive/inexpensive c'est cher/pas cher
do you take credit cards? acceptez-vous des cartes de credit?
I need a doctor/dentist j'ai besoin d'un médecin/dentiste
can you help me? pouvez-vous m'aider?
where is the hospital? où est l'hôpital?
where is the police station? où est le commissariat?

INDEX

A

Acclimatation, Jardin d' 58
accommodations 62–65
airport tax 89
airports 88, 89
Alexandre III, Pont 55
Alma, Pont de l' 55
André-Citroën, Parc 56
Arab Institute 45
Arc de Triomphe 27, 57
architecture, 20th-century 54
Arènes de Lutèce 59
Armée, Musée de l' 28
art and antique shops 77
Art Moderne de la Ville de Paris, Musée d' 50
Arts, Pont des 55
Arts d'Afrique et d'Océanie, Musée National des 51
Arts Décoratifs, Musée des 34
Astérix, Parc 58
auction rooms 59
Aubry, Martine 9

B

Bagatelle, Parc de 56
Balabus 19
Balzac, Maison de 50
banks 89
bars 84–85
Bastille 18
Batobus 19
bed and breakfast 65
Bibliothèque de France 54
Bir-Hakeim, Pont de 55
boat trips 19
Bois de Boulogne 56
Boulevard de Rochechouart 60
Bourdelle, Antoine 50
brasseries and bistros 72, 73
bridges 55
buses 91

C

Café Beaubourg 53
Café de Flore 53
Café Marly 53
cafés 53
canal trips 19
Carnavalet, Musée 46

Centre Georges Pompidou 41
Champs Élysées 27
Charles de Gaulle, Pont 55
Chasse, Musée de la 16
Chazal, Claire 9
children's activities 58
Chirac, Jacques 9
church concerts 82
churches 52, 90
Cinéma, Musée du 25
cinemas 85
Cirque Alexis Grüss 58
Cité de la Musique 54
Cité des Sciences et de l'Industrie 50
La Closerie des Lilas 53
Cluny, Musée de 38
concert venues 82
Conciergerie 40
Cour Carrée 18
Cour de Rohan 60
credit cards 89
crime 92
currency exchange 89
customs regulations 88
cycling 19

D

De Gaulle, Charles 12
Delacroix, Musée 60
Les Deux Magots 53
Disneyland Paris 58
Dôme, Église du 28
Drouot Richelieu 59

E

Egyptian obelisk 30
Eiffel Tower 26
electricity 90
embassies and consulates 93
emergencies 92–93
Équipages, Musée des 21
etiquette 89–90
events 22
excursions 20–21

F

fashion shops 74–5
flea markets 42
food and drink 53, 66–73, 84–85
free attractions 59

G

Gaessler, Carole 9
Gagnaire, Pierre 9
Galerie Colbert 36
Galerie Vivienne 36
galleries, commercial 77
Gaultier, Jean-Paul 9
La Géode 58
Giverny 20, 21
Grand Palais 27
La Grande Arche 54
La Grande Roue 57
Gustave Moreau, Musée 50–51

H

Hébert, Musée 60
Histoire Naturelle, Muséum National d' 51
history 10–12
Homme, Musée de l' 25
hotels 62–65
Hugo, Victor 7, 47

I

Île Saint-Louis 44
Institut du Monde Arabe 45
Les Invalides 28
itineraries 14–15

J

jazz clubs 82–83
Jeu de Paume 30

L

language (basic vocabulary) 93
Latin Quarter 17
lost property 92
Louvre, Musée du 35
Luxembourg, Jardin du 37

M

Maison Européenne de la Photographie 50
Maison du Verre 54
Maison Victor Hugo 47
maps 91
Marché aux Puces de Saint-Ouen 42
Marie, Pont 55
Marine, Musée de la 25

markets 42, 76
Marmottan, Musée 24
medical treatment 92
Mémorial de la
    Déportation 59
métro 90–91
Monceau, Parc 56
Monet, Claude 21
money 89
Montsouris, Parc 56
Monuments Français,
    Musée des 25
Moreau, Gustave 50–51
La Mosquée 52
museums and galleries
    50–51, 89

N
Napoleon Bonaparte 12,
    28
National Archives 16
national holidays 89
Neuf, Pont 55
newspapers 92
nightclubs 83
Notre Dame 43

O
opening hours 89
opera 82
Opéra de Paris 32
Orangerie 30
Orsay, Musée d' 31

P
Palais Bourbon 30
Palais de Chaillot 25
Palais de la Découverte 27
Palais de Justice 59
Palais-Royal, Jardin du 59
Panthéon Bouddhique
    (Guimet), Musée du
    51
Parisians 9
parks and gardens 56
passports and visas 88
Pavillon de l'Arsenal 59
Père Lachaise, Cimetière
    du 48
Petit Palais 27
Petit Trianon 21
pharmacies 92
Picasso, Musée 51
Place de la Concorde 30
Place des Vosges 47
places of worship 52, 90

pollution 57
Porte Dauphine 54
post offices 89, 92
public transportation 14,
    90–91
puppet shows 58

Q
Quai d'Anjou 44

R
radio and television 92
rail services 88
rented accommodations 65
restaurants 66–73
river buses 14
Rodin, Musée 29
Royal, Parc 16
Royal, Pont 55
Rue du Cherche-Midi 60
Rue Jacob 60
Rue Mallet-Stevens 54
Rue Monsieur-le-Prince
    60
Rue des Rosiers 60
Rue Vavin 54
Rue Vieille-du-Temple 60

S
Sacré Coeur 33
Sainte Chapelle 39
Sainte-Croix-de-Paris,
    Cathédrale 16
Saint-Etienne-du-Mont,
    Église 52
Saint-Eustache, Église de
    52
Saint-Germain-des-Prés,
    Église de 52
Saint-Louis, Église 28
Saint-Merri, Église de 52
Saint-Pierre 33
Saint-Séverin, Église de
    52
Saint-Sulpice, Église de
    52
La Samaritaine 57
seasons 88
Seine 18
Sens, Hôtel de 17
Serres d'Auteuil, Jardin
    des 56
shopping 74–81
Sinclair, Anne 9
sport 86
Square du Vert Galant 57

Starck, Philippe 9
statistics 8
steambaths 85
student travelers 90
swimming-pools 86

T
taxis 91
tea rooms 53
Techniques, Musée
    National des 51
telephone numbers,
    emergency 92–93
telephones 91
theme parks 58
time differences 90
toilets 90
Tour Eiffel 26
Tour Montparnasse 57
Tourist Information
    Office 90
tours, guided 19
travel insurance 89
travel passes 91
traveling to Paris 88–89
Tuileries, Jardin des 56

V
Vaux-le-Vicomte 20–21
Versailles 20
views of Paris 57
Village Saint-Paul 17

W
walks 16–18, 19
women travelers 90

Citypack
Paris

Important note

Time inevitably brings changes, so always confirm prices, travel facts, and other perishable information when it matters. Although Fodor's cannot accept responsibility for errors, you can use this guide in the confidence that we have taken every care to ensure its accuracy.

Published in the United States by Fodor's Travel Publications, Inc.
Published in the United Kingdom by AA Publishing

Fodor's is a registered trademark of Random House, Inc.

ISBN 0–679–00511–0
Third Edition 1999

FODOR'S CITYPACK PARIS

         AUTHOR *Fiona Dunlop*
         REVISER *Elisabeth Morris, Mario Wyn-Jones*
         COVER DESIGN *Tigist Getachew, Fabrizio La Rocca*
         INDEXER *Marie Lorimer*

Acknowledgments

The Automobile Association would like to thank the following photographers, picture libraries and associations for their assistance in the preparation of this book: BRIDGEMAN ART LIBRARY 34, carpet decorated with animals, wool and needlepoint (Musée des Arts Décoratifs, Paris); F. DUNLOP 44b, 45; THE LOUVRE 35b; MUSÉE CARNAVALET 46a; 34; MUSÉE MARMOTTAN 24; REX FEATURES LTD 9.
All remaining pictures are held in the Association's own library (AA PHOTO LIBRARY), with contributions from: M. ADLEMAN 87a; P. ENTICKNAP 26b; R. MOORE 21; D. NOBLE 20; K. PATERSON 2, 5a, 5b, 6, 25a, 25b, 28a, 28b, 30, 39a, 40, 43a, 52, 53, 56, 60; B. RIEGER 1, 17, 23a, 32, 44a, 55, 57, 58, 61b; A. SOUTER 7, 13a, 16, 18, 26a, 27, 29, 31a, 31b, 41b, 43b, 48, 49a, 50, 51, 54; W. VOYSEY 13b, 23b, 33a, 35a, 36a, 36b, 41a, 42, 46b, 47, 49b, 59, 61a, 87b. The author would like to thank Dominique Benedittini, Christophe Boicos and Andrew Hartley for their help during the preparation of this book.

Color separation by Daylight Colour Art Pte Ltd, Singapore
Manufactured by Dai Nippon Printing Co. (Hong Kong) Ltd

10 9 8 7 6 5 4 3 2 1

Titles in the Citypack series

● Amsterdam ● Atlanta ● Beijing● Berlin ● Boston ● Chicago ● Dublin ●
● Florence ● Hong Kong ● London ● Los Angeles ● Miami ● Montreal ●
● New York ● Paris ● Prague ● Rome ● San Francisco ● Seattle ● Shanghai ●
● Sydney ● Tokyo ● Toronto ● Venice ● Washington, D.C. ●